Embracing my Season

Discovering God's Grand Design for Your life

Stuart Webb

LAKESIDE PUBLISHING

Lakeside Publishing
P.O BOX 6219
Meridan Plains 4551
Queensland, Australia

My thanks to Nigel Baron and Alan Lilley for the hours of work spent on this project to make it look and read well. My thanks also to my wife Michelle and daughter Emma for their feedback and encouragement to believe in this book.

My prayer always that those who read this book would find themselves in Jesus. Sons and daughters of our great and wonderful God. Amen.

Contents

Prelude

One day I woke and said to myself,
If only I had more money, then I would be happy.
If only I could work less and spend more time with
the family, then I'd be happy.
Perhaps when I'm famous, then I'll be happy.
We just need a good holiday, then we'll be happy.
That day finished, and still I was not happy.
Another day I woke and said to myself,
Once I have greater respect in the workplace then
I'll be happy.
When my kids are happy then I'll be happy.
When I have my dream house, then I'll be happy.
When I retire, I'll be happy.
When I get that new job, then I'll be happy.
One day I woke and I had all these things and I still
wasn't happy.
Oh why oh why do I always want more.

Step by step we achieve these mystical happy places only to find the happiness is fleeting, and then our eyes turn to the next goal, project, or relationship. Why am I always left wanting more? Surely there is more to life than this? There must be something that can fill the emptiness I feel.

The pages of this book will unravel the rich meaning and purpose that can be found living 'in your season' while enjoying the relationships, challenges, and ambitions of life. Embracing your season isn't about a success culture or chasing after fleeting happiness. It's not about self-help and finding a belief system that meets your needs. Instead it is to be found in embracing the messy, complicated, beautiful season in which we live and discovering God's perfect plan for our season.

Read on and find out how.

Introduction
Finding Balance

Help!!!!!! Why do I struggle to find balance in my life?
My wife, Michelle and I have four children who are our greatest joy this side of heaven. They are constantly in our thoughts, in our prayers, and in our bank balances. We listen to their stories, follow their friendships, follow their Facebook pages for clues. (I try not to do this it unless there's a girlfriend/boyfriend on the scene.).

I remember the diaper changes at close range (dry retches) and the late night teething and trying to be the best parent I can be while constantly tired. Working full-time while juggling school drop-offs/pickups, soccer practice and music lessons.

Laughing at their jokes and hilarious antics, feeling the pain of their rejections and failures. Leaping for joy at their first places and awards. Squeezing in a date-night hoping not to fall asleep before 'happy hour' in the boudoir. So many great memories and more still to come.

Then there's the in-laws and the outlaws, the dramas, the fights and the laughter of sharing in the extended family life. Meeting the expectations of both sides of the family, or more likely failing to meet the expectations of both sides of the family.

Finding time in the calendar to attend Aunty Marge's 60th and the niece's Ballet recital in the morning. Just when we thought our personal life couldn't get crazier, our work is worse. The commute seems longer each day and the boss's body odour worse than ever.

Tomorrow's performance review, the list of KPI's, the grumpy memo from accounting, and all this in the name of the career.

This hectic, sometimes crazy, beautiful messy life is mine, and the good news is that it's mostly healthy despite the mess. If you're feeling stretched or out of balance, sometimes exhausted and overwhelmed, this doesn't automatically mean something is wrong.

This may well be the season you need to be in. In fact, I've yet to meet a healthy person who didn't find the child-raising years a rollercoaster ride … it's meant to be. This being said, it's important to acknowledge the difference between a healthy, beautiful, messy life and an unhealthy messy life.

The difference lies in whether we continue to thrive and grow or merely survive these years or worse, our life and our family life become a train wreck.

'Train wreck' or 'Beautifully messy'

Are you wondering which one your life is right now? If you describe it as beautifully messy, then you've already begun to embrace your season in a positive way. Either that or you're in denial, in which case life will soon become a train wreck. If you are unsure, the following chapters may shine a light on the truth for you.

If you're reading this and thinking in your heart, 'I'd love to believe it's beautifully messy, but honestly I think my life is a train wreck.' This does not mean that all areas of your life are a train wreck. Your marriage might be good, but your work life is a train wreck. Perhaps at work you feel your life is really well-balanced, but when you get home you feel completely out of control.

Perhaps your marriage is a train wreck, but your gym workouts keep getting better. Perhaps your whole life feels out of balance and it feels like each day you slide further into depression.

It's at this point that you need to hear me say, 'You are not alone, many feel as you do and we have a friend and ally waiting for us to call for help.'

Our Friend and Ally
Right from the start of this book I want to express my belief that 'self-help' is 'no help'. I, like most people, have read self-help books on parenting, time management, emotional well-being, marriage, empowerment and so on.

Some of these were presented by well-meaning Christian writers and others by 'Best Selling' authors. Ultimately their impact on my life was at best short-term. I would quickly return to 'out of balance'.

Was this because I lacked will-power or self-belief? Had my attitude or way of thinking caused me to stop speaking into reality what I hoped for? No. The reality of self-help is that it believes that the answers to finding balance, human frailty, human need, human longing for intimacy and acceptance are fulfilled by unlocking your own 'inner' power/strength/potential/conqueror.

All sorts of jargon are used, effectively encouraging us to climb the mountain in our own strength. In the experiences of my own beautiful messy life and in 20 years of journeying with thousands of other people in their beautiful messy lives, I have discovered a truth which sets apart the healthy from the unhealthy.

The great news is that it has little to do with 'self -help' and everything to do with allowing our Saviour and friend, our ally Jesus, to 'do life' with us. There is such a richness in discovering God's passionate plans for love, compassion, purpose, peace, service, and generosity for our lives. This book hopes to move us away from ideas of 'self-help' to 'partnership'.

I do not for one minute suggest we don't have to make a response or take responsibility for making good choices.

I would simply argue that taking responsibility and making good choices only becomes truly possible when we enter a partnership with the designer and creator of our masterpiece, the messy beautiful life we live.

I believe the Christian life is defined not by our journey to climb the mountain to God, but by the fact that our God climbed down the mountain to us so we journey together to amazing heights.

Chapter 1
Let's start at the beginning

A Grand Design

Most of us live our lives blissfully unaware that we are called to live a life with a grand design. We often embrace elements of this design without ever realising the bigger vision it is part of. Since ancient times, humans have been aware that there are forces at work in our world which are beyond our understanding.

We often came up with a multiplicity of deities and mysticisms to explain them, and certainly, in our modern scientific age, we use science to make sense of many of them. There is however a problem that even science struggles to grapple with.

How do we explain WHY we are here? We might theorise the HOW we are here - big bang theory and evolution, or perhaps intelligent design, but still the question remains, **'Why are we here'**? This, I believe, is a fundamental pursuit for human beings who wish to live by a grand design, searching for a life with genuine meaning and purpose now and indeed beyond this mortal coil.

My Grand Design.

At the grand old age of 11, I distinctly remember lying awake in my bed staring out the window at night and gazing at the stars and wondering, 'How did the stars get there? If God made the stars, then who made God?' Perhaps this was the beginning of my own awareness that my story was part of a bigger one. None of the adults in my life seemed to have a very good answer to my questions, but I never really gave up on these questions.

Ultimately this thirst to understand who I was and where my story fitted into the universe led me to study for a Bachelor of Science degree at University. I studied evolution, microbiology, botany and chemistry, biochemistry and anything else that I thought might hold some answers to my questions. I decided early on I wasn't gifted as a physicist, yet my love for it continues to this day. Out of all the sciences I studied, physics wrestled best with the mystery of the grand design I saw at work around me. Still, over and over again my studies wrestled with 'How' the universe worked or how it came to be, but never the 'Why'.

Among my fellow students and even my lecturers there was an obsession with the 'How' but rarely was there any concern for the grander question of 'Why'.

Why am I here? What is the meaning of life? Why do all things, especially life, move towards order rather than chaos? Essentially, I hungered to understand the 'grand design' for the universe and my life.

This search for the grand design led me to some interesting places and ultimately, beyond the study only of science, and into philosophy and spirituality. I will talk more of my own search later in the book but if you are someone who knows deep in their bones that there is more to life than 'causality' and 'chance' then read on.

The Atheist's Problem

As a pastor, I find myself leading the final farewells for many of the people I care for and their families. At these funerals I am called on to lead a dignified remembrance of their life and help loved ones find solace and meaning in the big questions that death raises.

What's next? Is there life after death? Why did they die? Amongst other pertinent questions. Most people in grief are usually unable or unwilling to grapple with rational or logical explanations so I leave this to a wiser moment.

Indeed, I would argue that the logical, rational and empirical explanations of death are usually pretty much rubbish anyway. I believe the real answers are found in 'spiritual truth' rather than logic, empiricism or rationalism.

Ask most people what is true in their life and they will tell you - family, friends and love, not a developed evolutionary theory or quantum string theory.

As human beings, we instinctively find meaning in our relationships even if we've never articulated it. I would argue that the 'truth' in our lives is best articulated in the narrative/story. It is here that the source of all 'truth' is discovered when we understand that God's narrative and human history are entangled.

We cannot know the truth of our existence or our eternal destiny without understanding how we are all part of a long story that began with God and is fulfilled in his Son Jesus. It is starting from this place that I try to craft a sermon for each funeral.

One of my more memorable encounters was during a wake after celebrating the life of a person who was largely a stranger to me. Having not known the person well but in the knowledge that they were a person of faith I felt it right to reflect that faith in my sermon. During the wake I was approached by a well-dressed man (most are at a funeral) who engaged me about my sermon. His interest was so enthusiastic I made the mistake of assuming he was also a person who shared the deceased's faith. I had preached that the guiding force to faith was hope.

I said we are a people of hope. Society often mistakenly thinks we are a people of rules and rites, a people who think they have all the answers and sit in judgement of others for their failings. Rather, we are a people who leave judgement to God.

We are a people who freely acknowledge the absence of perfect understanding and knowledge of our God. Yet despite this, we speak of belief and trust in a perfect God who has a plan and a saviour for humanity in Jesus. Yes, we are a people of great hope. Hope for our present, hope for our future and a hope that life is eternal through faith in Jesus.

My well-dressed friend said, 'I've never heard religion referred to as "defined by hope" before'. Our conversation around the hope of humanity was going so well that I asked, 'Do you worship here on the Coast?' He smiled and pulled out his card, 'President Atheist Society'. I nearly fell over.

I now understood his interest. For an atheist all things are reduced to 'chance'. All the laws of the universe, all theories of life and humanity's place in it boil down to pure chance. Gravity is a governing law of the universe yet in reality even it is a matter of chance. When I get out of bed in the morning the only reason I plant my feet on the ground and not float into the clouds is because of the constant governing law of the universe called 'Gravity'.

Yet if even gravity is governed by chance then I should have no expectation that it will still be operating tomorrow. The simple truth is that an atheist, whether they admit it or not, wakes up hoping gravity is still operating.

So what is the greater truth - 'chance' or 'hope'? You see, I believe there is more truth found in the narrative of humanity's relationship to God than there is in chance.

The Christian story is that a God who is beyond our imagining, beyond our logic, beyond our philosophy, beyond our scientific knowledge created a universe that only we are able to stand in awe of.

No other species studies the stars, unravels the governing laws of the universe. No other species can live in awe and wonder at the world in which we live. Perhaps the most outrageous claim of Christians is that this same God became human so that we would not only live in wonder but that we would live in relationship with this God.

The well-dressed man and I had a memorable conversation and agreed next time he was on the Coast we would meet for coffee. (We haven't yet.)

Wonder and Awe
But we still don't know the meaning of life…or do we?

In our modern world we often rather arrogantly believe we are thinking things never thought out before, that our scientific age has made us more enlightened. In some respects, I would argue that this is true; however, when it comes to the question of 'Why am I here?', I would argue that we are standing on the shoulders of giants to answer this question today.

One such giant is found in a very ancient text 'The first Book of Kings' where we see the chronicles of a King named Solomon, arguably one of the best documented and famous kings of antiquity.

Solomon was renowned for his wisdom and teaching as well as wealth and military success.

I can't recall too many Kings whose wisdom teaching lives on to this day. Solomon authored a book called 'Ecclesiastes' also known as 'The search for happiness under the sun'. His book details his attempt to find meaning for his life.

Being a King he had unlimited power and wealth and applied himself to gaining every advantage this could afford. He pursued every pleasure he could think of with wives and concubines, food, drink and parties. Solomon also applied himself to scholarly pursuit in the hope it would bring him meaning. He chased wealth and gained it so that he was the richest King of his time.

After a lifetime pursuing all wealth, knowledge and pleasure he recorded his simple discovery about the meaning of life.

Its simplicity is a little unnerving and challenging, so what was it? Solomon discovered a Grand Design to his life, one he wished he could have realised when younger and applied its lessons earlier.

Most of us reading this book live in a time of unparalleled wealth something more akin to Solomon himself.

In many ways we live like kings, in some ways even better than the kings of antiquity with access to better health care and fresh food options thanks to refrigeration and pleasures brought by technology.

When it comes to the pursuit of knowledge, again we have access to far greater scholarly material than ever in history.

When it comes to pleasure we have more disposable income to spend on pleasure and thanks to the modern media we are bombarded with a steady stream of purchases that will make us 'happy'.

So despite the fact that we are modern day Kings and Queens in pursuit of a Grand Design for our lives we still can't find it in our wealth, knowledge or pleasure pursuits.

So does it exist and if so, where do I find it?

Chapter 2
My season

Life is Messy

Let's be honest now. Our lives are complicated and messy and that's how it's supposed to be. This is different to saying it's out of control or ugly. It's in the messy that we find richness, it's in the complicated that we find meaning. Now you're asking what on earth does he mean?

Embracing the season

King Solomon wrote

For everything there is a season, and a time for every matter under heaven:
a time to be born, and a time to die;
a time to plant, and a time to pluck up what is planted;
a time to kill, and a time to heal;
a time to break down, and a time to build up;
a time to weep, and a time to laugh;
a time to mourn, and a time to dance;
a time to throw away stones, and a time to gather stones together;
a time to embrace, and a time to refrain from embracing;
a time to seek, and a time to lose;
a time to keep, and a time to throw away;
a time to tear, and a time to sew;
a time to keep silence, and a time to speak;
a time to love, and a time to hate;
a time for war, and a time for peace. (NRSV)

There is a saying, 'Life is what happens while we are busy making plans'. There is a truth to this which speaks of our experience of life. We wake up one day and the years have passed and we wonder where they went.

It wasn't that we didn't have goals and plans; it's just that life gets busy and one day rolls into another. However, waking up and seeing that we spent our life well should be a priority. There is nothing sadder than a life wasted.

I have the good fortune to lead a group of men who have a commitment to each other to meet regularly; we call it the 'Man Cave'. Our motto is to live as if 'Our life counts'. Many of us are men with wives and children of school age and younger, and our lives are in the busiest season we will ever know. Between school sport, instrumental groups, lawns, careers, bills to pay, community commitments, we are stretched in every way.

Our desire is to make it all count. We do not want to wake up one day and realise in the busyness we lost sight of the meaning and purpose, not to mention the Joy. We desire to be good fathers to children who respect themselves as well as others.

Treat our wives in such a manner that they will still want to be with us once the kids leave. Build careers on integrity not just on achievement.

Essentially we want to embrace the season in which we live and make it count. My wife Michelle is a physiotherapist and community leader, an impressive athlete and good looking on top of it all. Ask her what the most important part of her season is and she will tell you to be a mother to our four children. This defining element to her season means she finds daily purpose in even the mundane tasks of raising a family.

So…how do I know what season I'm in?

King Solomon gives us a philosophical look at our seasons but how would you describe your season? What projects define your season? Are you happy in your season or are you trying to survive it? Who are the most important people in your season?

Perhaps the most important question we have to ask ourselves is, 'What is my season'? And equally, 'What is the most defining role or project to this season'. For each of us our lives are unique in many ways yet when we scratch the surface they are not as unusual as we might think.

In my current role as a Pastor and community leader I began to see some common seasons amongst the people I journeyed with. Sometimes I would be listening to someone tell me of their struggles and think, 'Wow - I'm listening to myself'.

Although the details of our seasons vary there are some distinct qualities, struggles and paths forward if we do the work of defining and embracing our current season.

The following seasons are best understood as metaphors to help real people define real lives in a way that helps them embrace and thrive, not just survive their season.

My 'Winter of Discontent'

I love winter. I love snuggling into my Duvet on cold nights, it's even better when my wife is there to snuggle with. I love reading in front of the fireplace, and long walks without a drop of sweat. When I'm in snow I love the squeal of children playing in it and if I get the chance to ski in it...look out. There is a lot to love about winter when we embrace it.

Of course for some of us winter is a time of great discontent. It's just too cold, I always get sick, my bones ache in the cold. Some of us endure the winter desperate for the spring that is around the corner. So it is with those who cannot embrace their season 'Winter of Discontent'. The most common season I see people live in is the 'Winter of Discontent'.

You'll know you're in this season if you are constantly anxious, constantly exhausted, depressed by your life's circumstances. Life is busy and the demands on you are overwhelming. The kids want more of you than you have to give, the boss is expecting your best, your partner seems to be struggling as much as you and you feel less and less like lovers and more like business partners in raising the family.

Your health suffers and you catch every bug going around. If this is you there's good news. The fix is as simple as 'embracing your season'. Not excited about this fix, relax - it's better than you think.

My Restless Autumn

Autumn is a beautiful season. I remember living in New Zealand in my mid-twenties and visiting a little place called Arrowtown. It was lined with beautiful old beechwood and maple-leaf trees whose leaves would turn spectacular shades of red and purple, pink and yellow and brown.I remember that first hint of cool breeze and the ebbing of the summer heat. In Autumn I have this strong sense of expectancy that things are changing. The changeover in sports and the starting of Rugby and soccer season - ooohhh so good.

In working with 20 to 30 year olds I'm discovering an increasing number of young people battling a hopelessness often treated as depression. It is not limited to this group but prevalent here in my experience.

Those in the 'restless autumn' understand that they are privileged. They know they are well off, often having good marriages or partners, and well paid jobs. They have many ways to find pleasure, and have many modern toys and a plethora of ways to interact socially with their peers.

Yet despite all this and knowing they are fortunate they express a sense of hopelessness that none of it means anything and that there should be more to their life but they can't see it, can't visualise it getting any better.

Some seek ever riskier behaviour to capture greater meaning, some turn to drugs and alcohol abuse (mostly in a social context at first) in seeking experiences that make them feel more alive.

I hasten to add that none of these behaviours are new nor limited to the young. However, there is a growing dissatisfaction with what they perceive as the status quo of previous generations. I believe there are some obvious risk factors we can associate with this growing 'Restless Autumn'.

Perpetual Summer

It's just so hot, it's too hot, I can't handle it. Where I come from, Summer can be pretty Hot and seems to extend beyond summer's boundaries. For me it's when I dust off my surf board and enjoy the sun and salt on my skin, unfortunately when I also sustain the most injuries. If you're reading this in a cold climate, then Summer might be the season we long for and many good memories are made in summer.

This season encompasses those trapped by the past, but holds the key to the future. Sometimes things that happen in our past can enslave our future. It can seem impossible to escape our upbringing, our culture but even harder to escape the hurts of our past. How do you know if this might be your season?

If you're reading this and past relationships hold you back from making the most of your current ones; if you suffered abuse as a child and it's still preventing you from having meaningful intimacy and trust; if your pattern of friendship is conflict and breakup; if your identity is defined by past hurts, then this season is you.

Why summer? I described summer by saying it's 'just so hot'. People in the summer season when they talk about the past say things like, 'I'll never forgive him for what he did to me', 'That's just how it is', 'I can't change', 'You just have to accept me as I am', 'Why should I trust you everyone else has let me down'.

People who love you describe you as 'closed off', 'emotionally distant', 'guarded'. You say of yourself, 'I don't let people in', 'I find people hard to trust, even those that love me'.

Before you put your walls up even to this book please understand that embracing your season is the key to your future's purpose. This is not judging you and you mustn't condemn yourself for the past and its lasting effect on you, but you mustn't remain its prisoner.

My 'Indifferent Spring'

I love spring! For me spring means I'm not getting up in the dark anymore. Without even trying I just seem to get a new 'spring' in my step when spring arrives. In my family it signifies holidays are around the corner and I'm usually hunting around for a new camping spot to take the family. With the start of the warmer weather I can coax my sometimes resistant teenagers to part with their cosy beds for a camp stretcher.

I enjoy the camp fires and long conversations during bush walks, the board games at night and waking up to the sound of birds. For me my 'Spring' associations are all about love and family, change and hopefulness.

Spring is that wonderful time of year when all things become new. Spring signifies new beginnings, new birth, colour, and new warmth.

If you're living in a cold climate then spring signifies an end to the cold, an end to the short days, and blossoming of new life. Spring should speak to us about new possibilities, new opportunities, a revitalised sense of our future.

Spring is a call to embrace change and to take a new optimistic approach to our lives, our relationships and our tomorrows. This is not the case for someone travelling through an 'Indifferent Spring'.

If you are living in an 'Indifferent Spring' you have chosen not to embrace change, new possibilities. You cling to the same way of living because it's what you know, it's safe, it feels comfortable even if it's dysfunctional. It's spring outside and you are surrounded by God-given opportunities for growth yet you are indifferent to them.

Living in an 'Indifferent Spring' is the greatest nemesis to growth. For most of us as we age we become more set in our ways of thinking and behaving. We also shrink in our willingness to care about others and the world in which we live. Perhaps it is born of a world weariness or perhaps that's just the excuse we use. My suspicion is that for many of us it's a product of 'My Indifferent Spring'. What I mean to say is we have become increasingly comfortable with the 'little' world we've created. Perhaps you've retired and are financially comfortable.

Perhaps you have decided it's too hard to make new friends or have new experiences because you've become so comfortable with the ones you have (or lack of, in some cases). Perhaps remaining single means you can indulge your own needs and not have to worry about pleasing another. Either way you have 'Settled' for less and become comfortable with mediocre.

You make statements like, 'This is just how I am, like it or lump it', 'It's in my genes, my father was the same way'. You switch off to anything that makes you uncomfortable and you avoid suffering even when it's necessary.

Why 'My Indifferent Spring'? While around us there is new life and growth, abundant Joy and possibility, my life has become unchanging. There is no growth, no new life. One day is the same as the next; it's comfortably boring. I no longer ask the big questions of life (if I ever did). Why am I here? Where do I find meaning and purpose? What happens to me when I die? Is there more to life than this?

How do you know if this is you? Well, your response to these questions is 'Indifferent', it doesn't matter or there is no answer.

You've settled. If this is you and you're still reading, stick with it. Yours is perhaps the most exciting transformation of all if you're willing.

My 'off-peak' season

I love to Ski. I enjoy the thrill of flying down the mountain at break-neck speed. The cold fresh air in your face. These are usually where I gather my best skiing stories from, because they involve spectacular crashes and stories of courage that grow more dramatic with each telling. I also enjoy navigating technically difficult passages slowly but practicing those skills (not my speciality).

Of course what's not to love about hot mulled wine on the mountain and sitting in front of the fireplace at night? Unfortunately skiing is also an expensive pastime so when I have managed to go skiing it's usually been during the 'off-peak season' which means outside school holidays.

Snow can be a bit hit or miss at these times but I've been pretty fortunate in the past. It usually means fewer people and less wait times on chairlifts, and the way I ski it also means fewer people to run into on the mountain.

Those who travel in the off-peak season aren't afraid to take a calculated risk or explore beyond their means.

The off-peak season invites new possibilities for those who seek wise counsel and the courage to embrace the season.

Some of us reading this book have read all the seasons and decided we don't identify with any of them. This is entirely possible but unlikely; perhaps you were trying to identify with the characters so re-reading the introduction to each season might help. However, if you are amongst the few who don't identify with the four seasons it might mean you are 'off-peak'. You aren't travelling where the pack travels or perhaps you were once in one of the four seasons but moved beyond them.

A note of caution is required here because some of us may arrive in this season because of a lack of self-reflection or worse, narcissism. What is the off-peak season? The off - peak season is a time of transition, an unsettled place or time.

Perhaps you've decided change is required but are not sure which direction to take. It's important to know you are not trying to escape your season but just feel within yourself there is something else for you to do. Effectively the season is changing. How do you know if your season is 'off-peak?

Your life and relationships are working okay and there are no crises. You're not unhappy but you're restless. Perhaps an opportunity has been knocking at your door but you are uncertain. Your significant relationships (spouse, best friends, parents) sense your restlessness and you increasingly have the same conversation with them about what you've been thinking you might or would like to do. Despite their best efforts you don't take their advice. You regularly make statements like, 'I'd like to but I'm not sure', 'I'm ready for change but don't know what to do'.

So which Season am I?
Take some time to identify which of these seasons feel like you. Perhaps it feels like you are between a couple of them. Either way being honest with yourself and about where you really are are the keys to making the most of your life now rather than some magical future happiness. Underline or scribble a note underneath your season and say, 'If I'm honest this is me'. This might be a painful realisation or it may be liberating. The good news is your present is about to change for the better.

If you are struggling to pin down your season, talk with someone you trust who knows you well and talk it through with them. Either way there are some challenges that are common to us all and will help us embrace our season. Let's get started.

Let's begin with our stress and anxiety. Let's identify the pressure points and triggers in our life. We tend to talk about stress and anxiety in negative terms.

Certainly long term unchecked high levels lead to some serious health issues, however these are natural responses designed to point us toward meaningful achievement and drive positive ambition.

Understanding that if we are feeling overwhelmed and we start to get sick then our body is trying to tell us something. If we are increasingly feeling depressed by our circumstances, then they're pointing us toward change either in our attitude or in those circumstances.

Jesus was quoted as saying, '*Therefore I tell you, do not worry about your life, what you will eat or what you will drink; or about your body, what you will wear. Is not life more than food, and the body more than clothing? Look at the birds of the air; they neither sow nor reap nor gather into barns, and yet your heavenly Father feeds them. Are you not of more value than they? And can any of you by worrying add a single hour to your span of life? Matthew 6:25-27 (NRSV).*

It seems our worry is not a new thing. Jesus said this over 2000 years ago. The moral of this saying is simple, 'How do you value your life?' Is your life valued by your possessions and achievements? Do you waste your life worrying about the material things of life rather than the truly meaningful things like our relationships with others?

Where to now?

Hopefully you're a little closer to understanding the season you're in. If you are not, don't worry. As you continue reading it will become clearer. If you are pretty convinced you know your season, then let's begin looking at how we can embrace it and find Joy in it rather than just angst. Understanding and embracing your season is the key to finding peace in our lives and a sense of purpose and meaning in our challenges and triumphs. Let's start with our hunger.

Chapter 3

I hunger

When you read this title I wonder if you thought of food or if it elicited an emotional response. Hunger on a practical level we associate with food, but at emotional level we associate it with desire, need, longing. Truth be told, 'HUNGER' is a normal part of human physiology in all its forms. Our Bodies tell us when we are hungry for food, our hormones are triggered in response to desire and need and our emotions gnaw away at us in longings. So it's safe to say that HUNGER is a constant state for humans. In saying this there is healthy HUNGER and unhealthy. I would go further and say there is appropriate hunger and inappropriate hunger or perhaps misaligned or confused hunger.

Once again our hunger can be in balance or out of balance and its effect on our life is significant.

For both men and women understanding our HUNGER and how to meet its call in healthy and life-giving ways will decide our capacity to live a life with a Grand Design.

Hunger varies across individuals and is often different for men and women although sometimes the line is blurry.

Typically, men hunger for sexual intimacy or sexual pleasure, power and or fame either for influence, control or strengthening the ego, wealth to project success and gain pleasure or experience. Some men hunger for knowledge so as to express both themselves and embrace their reality.

Men hunger for love but it is rarely articulated as 'love'; it tends to be a mix of desire, belonging, intimacy and purpose. It's just simpler to say 'love' which expresses also the sense of devotion men often feel towards those they love.

These of course are generalisations and indeed simplifications of a truly complex emotion and response.

For women Hunger often expresses itself as a desire for emotional and physical intimacy, security and belonging. The desire to nurture is often stronger in women and can be seen in the hunger for a child of their own.

Women often express a greater hunger to express their emotions to make sense of them or manage them. Women can also express a hunger for power or fame. Also to control, influence and strengthen the ego. A subtle difference between men and women is that fame is more associated with validation of personal appearance in strengthening the ego. You could argue these are social constructs, and again are generalisations.

Women also hunger for wealth but less for validation and more for security and in the same way as it is for men they use it for pleasure. Love is a significant hunger for women and they are often better at articulating what this means for them. Once again these are generalisations and women can often have complex combinations of these hungers. This is not designed to be an exhaustive list.

Why this long conversation about hunger? Because often we are unaware of our internal hungers even when they express themselves in our lives. Sometimes we can confuse one hunger with another.

Hunger for wealth
At this point I want to turn our eyes toward our hunger for wealth. More than any other *Hunger* I am witness to its destructive power. Every day, people from every walk of life are falling victim to an unhealthy fixation on wealth creation.

I say unhealthy because money of itself is neutral to our 'Grand Design'; however, if it is at the heart of our life we are heading for a very steep cliff. I count myself privileged to journey with so many people and I hope you will read this chapter understanding my desire to see people prosper.

For me to prosper means to have our hunger for wealth subject to our 'God's Grand Design' not our 'Grand Design' focused on our hunger for Wealth.

Even as I write this book I am using my breaks to walk the streets of where I'm staying and I find myself hungry for a house with such a view and such an entertaining area. Then I'm wondering what their lives are like, whether their Grand Design led to such prosperity or whether their Grand Design was this prosperity.

For those responding, 'What's the difference'? - one involves reward for achieving a higher purpose with a greater sense of meaning; the other possibly at the price of a marriage, estranged children, poor health, those we exploited. Big Difference.

A simple Truth in the face of Hunger

I began this chapter by saying that 'Hunger' is a normal part of human existence. The simple truth is that most of our lives exhibit a strong mix of healthy and unhealthy hunger. Some hungers are met with normal or healthy responses and others are met with self- destructive habits or responses. We need to take an honest journey at this point and ask, 'What hungers do I have in my life, and how do I fill them'?

In my own life I have had a battle with my weight and my sense of self-worth. These are very real hungers which in the past I was ill-informed to meet in heathy ways.

I am pleased to say that as I write this God has taken me on a healing journey in which he continues to meet the hungers which I once channelled into food and pleasure seeking.

So allow me to invite you into the journey of discovery which liberated me from slavery to food and pleasure and into health and an unquenchable belief in my self -worth, my God-worth. It began with a simple exercise, one which I invite you also to take.

'What is it that I hunger for in my life'? - Take five minutes to write down everything you hunger for. For me I hungered for self-worth, meaning, purpose, health, prosperity, love, belonging, fun.

'In which of these am I meeting my hunger in healthy ways'? - For me I had found healthy ways to meet my hunger for meaning, purpose, prosperity, love, belonging. Your turn...

'In which of these hungers am I living in unhealthy ways'? - For me my health suffered because I ate to manage stress/anxiety and when I struggled with my self-worth. My associations with fun were also too often met by food or escaping the reality of a life out of balance. I often tried to meet my hunger for self-worth in seeking approval from others (this is a fickle master). Your turn...

What are the consequences of continuing with this unhealthy hunger management?

For me it meant Yo-Yo dieting, constantly believing that food and exercise were the solution and the problem. The consequences if I hadn't been transformed were chronic health problems, ongoing self-worth problems. I would never have set a vision for my life and most certainly never have reached it. The consequences for me of staying in an unhealthy hunger were an-unfulfilled life, living with regret and chronic health problems. Being dependent on others for my self-worth meant spending my life swinging between exaltation and despair. Your turn…..

If it's not already obvious to us, then let me make it plain, 'There is a lot of pain associated with unhealthy hunger management'. It was always easier to reach for a doughnut than it was to face the necessary changes I'd need to make to deal effectively with my stress. It was easier to associate fun with food than it was with achievement. It was easier to hide in my poor self-worth than to trust in the promises of God. It was painful every time I'd try to change my life, painful to trust God, painful to face my fears.

It is much easier to stay comfortably entrenched in patterns of thinking and living that although destructive were (I believed) free from pain. The simple truth was…I was wrong, my understanding was wrong, my choices were wrong, my present and my future stories were wrong. Now that's a painful realisation.

Some of us reading this might be thinking, 'I believe you', but I've tried to change in the past and failed. I've tried to think differently; I've tried getting help. It works for a while but then I fall back into what I know. I hear you…that was me over and over again. I read the books, I applied my mind, I mustered my self-discipline and prayed and prayed for God's help. So what was different this time?

It's not JUST about YOU - that's the problem.

The reason we try and fail is because it requires more than your will-power and more than your mental faculties to bring about the change we need in our lives.

All of us have a 'broken-ness about our lives', it looks different for all of us but it's different sides of the same coin. For the longest time I hated my stomach because it reminded me every day of how I was failing to live the life I wanted to live.

It came as a great revelation to my life when I saw my protruding stomach for what it was… a gift. My stomach preceded me everywhere I went and served as a reminder that there was a tremendous opportunity to bring about life-altering changes. I began to thank God that changes in my health and the visible presence of my stomach were God's call to change. However, this time, 'NOT IN MY OWN STRENGTH'.

I began to realise that my struggles with self-worth were because I was looking for it in the wrong places and began to thank God for the strength of my emotions, the strength of my stress and anxiety and what they were screaming at me, 'You can't do it on your own', 'You need more than the opinion of others'.

Remember God has *'wonderfully and fearfully made you'* *Psalm 139:14 (NRSV),* and your design is to live in peace with Jesus the author and perfector of your faith.

When your car is broken you go to a mechanic, when your arm is broken you go to a doctor, when our soul is injured where do we go? I believe the cause of our unhealthy expressions of hunger are life's hurts and distortions caused by our and others' sin as it impacts our life.

The solution is to turn to the healing power of the one who created and sustains us. We are 'God-breathed' and are unable to sustain life everlasting without God's ongoing presence and healing. Are you ready to change everything? Let's start by understanding who we are.

'You are God-Breathed'

When we seek to explain who we are (our sense of identity), we often turn to our roles, father/mother, a husband/wife, friend, etc. These roles certainly form part of our identity but I would argue are not the whole story. Who am I? I might say I'm an artist or an athlete but once again this is what we are good at, not who we are. So I ask again, 'Who am I'?

This is a tough question and we invariably slide into roles/abilities and dualities to explain ourselves. Part of our problem in identifying our identity is our failure to acknowledge our true origins, in not making reference to our parents but to the very author and life giver of our true self, 'God-Breathed'.

In the book of Genesis chapter 1 verses 26-28 in the Bible it places our identity firmly in its origins.

Then God said, "Let us make man in our image, after our likeness. And let them have dominion over the fish of the sea and over the birds of the heavens and over the livestock and over all the earth and over every creeping thing that creeps on the earth."
So God created man in his own image,
in the image of God he created him;
male and female he created them.
And God blessed them. And God said to them, "Be fruitful and multiply and fill the earth and subdue it, and have dominion over the fish of the sea and over the birds of the heavens and over every living thing that moves on the earth. (ESV)

Then again in the second chapter of Genesis in verse 7 it says,

'then the Lord God formed the man of dust from the ground and breathed into his nostrils the breath of life, and the man became a living creature.'

At this point some of us might be tempted to get into arguments over Genesis as literal or metaphor, or evolution verses creation or science versus faith. Can I encourage us rather to hear what the writer is saying about God and our connection to him?

We can understand our identity as 'made in God's image', 'blessed by God', 'male and female', 'God Breathed'. Consequently, when I'm asked who I am I could say,

I am God-breathed, made in his image, and blessed. Because of this I am able to love as a father/mother daughter/son, husband/wife, friend. I reflect God in my creativity and athletic potential and in the freedom of will that I possess.

This truth if we embrace it can begin to breathe fresh life into our souls. Our self-worth can then be based on the knowledge that, *'I am fearfully and wonderfully made'* Psalm 139:14(NRSV).

When I put my trust in Jesus I became part of *'a chosen race, a royal priesthood, a holy nation...God's people'* 1 Peter 2:9-10 (NRSV).

When we live in the righteousness of Jesus, God says, 'I *will make my dwelling among you, and my soul shall not abhor you. And I will walk among you and will be your God, and you shall be my people' Leviticus 26:11-12 (ESV).*

Understanding that we were created to live in relationship with God, live with his very breath in our lungs and manifest his life-giving and creative potential in our lives can change everything.

No matter what hurt you've experienced, no matter how gifted or humble your talents, no matter what you look like or how popular or unpopular you are...you are called to be a child of God, designed to live in the light, and experience God's blessing.

Now all of this requires a response from us. We do not earn God's favour, nothing we do, no good deed, no pilgrimage, no self-sacrifice can merit God's friendship.

It is found in only one place, 'Jesus' the Christ. God loved us and recognised our inability to live without him. Even though we are determined to live without him the consequence is hate and fear, war and poverty, suffering and discord, a life decided by chance rather than destiny. Despite this the grace of our God destined that though we rejected him he did not reject us.

Instead God chose to send his son Jesus into the world to show us what love is. Jesus willingly gave his life on the cross to take our sin onto himself and destroy it. By taking our sins, our hate, our fear, our wrong thoughts, deeds and words onto himself it means that we are made whole again, made new.

Paul says in 2 Corinthians, *'Therefore, if anyone is in Christ, he is a new creation. The old has passed away; behold, the new has come.*
All this is from God, who through Christ reconciled us to himself and gave us the ministry of reconciliation; that is, in Christ God was reconciling the world to himself, not counting their trespasses against them, and entrusting to us the message of reconciliation (ESV).

This is good news for you and me because it means we are able to live under God's blessing free from our sin and suddenly all things can become new. Paul also writes that because of Jesus's presence in his life, *'I can do all things through him who strengthens me' (ESV).*
Ready to become a new creation? Ready to say goodbye to the mistakes of the past, the guilt, the regrets?
Ready to acknowledge that we are in need of a saviour? God's word teaches that we need only 'repent' and 'believe' Mark1:14-15.
Jesus has called you to this moment...stop and ask God's forgiveness for the wrongs of your past, ask God to heal the hurts. Jesus asks us to believe that he died on the cross for our sin and rose to life so that we too could live eternally. To repent means to 'change your mind' and act on what you believe. From this moment and for every future moment, decide to live your life with the living God present in it.

We know the living God in our lives through the death and resurrection of Jesus and the power of God's Spirit at work in us. Decide today to walk with Jesus the way we were designed from the beginning.

Here we gooooo!!!!! Tell a friend or a family member that you have decided to 'change your mind' and believe in Jesus for your everyday.

I'm just not good enough

For some of us we just aren't convinced yet. Maybe you're saying to yourself…if you knew me the way I KNOW me you would understand why I'm not good enough. I hear you and I can assure you you're not alone.

I've been a pastor for 20 years starting as a youth minister for 5 years and as an assistant minister for 2 years and running churches for 13 years. You'd think that with all these years of preaching, teaching and leading people I'd have understood the single biggest reason why people don't go to church…*I'm just not good enough.*

For all of these years of leading God's people one of my favourite messages was, 'None of us are good enough'.

That's the point, but God is good. I thought this was an awesome thing to tell people who didn't think they were good enough. This changed the day that one of my brand new Christian ladies said to me. 'You really freaked me out when I first heard you say that'. Thankfully I was intrigued not defensive so I inquired as to why. It seems I had for the last 20 years misunderstood the problem. People had no problem believing that they weren't good enough; instead, they had a great problem believing they were good enough for God to bother with. No it's not a play on words it's like turning over a fallen tree… out crawl the true nasties.

So now I say to people, 'you are good enough', because God is good. It actually makes more sense. Please hear me out on this one…If you weren't good enough for God why did he send Jesus to die on the cross for you? If you weren't good enough why did he build his church for you? If you weren't good enough why does God continue to bless your life with food and water and love and every other blessing in your life? If you weren't good enough, why did God ask me to write this book for you?

I know these reasons may not convince you either, but there is something important we all need to understand. That voice inside us that says we aren't good enough is not God's voice. In fact, it's not even your voice. It may sound like your mother or father or wife or husband or someone very powerful in your life…but it's not them either. Then who's voice is it that keeps accusing you that you're not good enough?

In the gospel of John chapter 8 there is a remarkable story of a woman caught in the act of adultery (very serious crime in Jesus's day, punishable by death) who is brought by religious leaders to Jesus to judge.

This was a trap set up to put Jesus against the Roman authorities of the day.

They made her stand before the group and said to Jesus,
"Teacher, this woman was caught in the act of adultery.
In the Law Moses commanded us to stone such women.
Now what do you say?" They were using this question as a
trap, in order to have a basis for accusing him.
But Jesus bent down and started to write on the ground
with his finger.
When they kept on questioning him, he straightened up and
said to them, "Let any one of you who is without sin be the
first to throw a stone at her."

Again he stooped down and wrote on the ground.
At this, those who heard began to go away one at a time,
the older ones first, until only Jesus was left, with the
woman still standing there. Jesus straightened up and
asked her, "Woman, where are they?
Has no one condemned you?"
"No one, sir," she said.
"Then neither do I condemn you," Jesus declared. "Go
now and leave your life of sin." (John 8: NIV)

Clearly this woman wasn't good enough, she was sinful, she had many accusers. Yet in the eyes of Jesus his desire was not to condemn her but to call her to change. Jesus desired to see her choose a better path rather than condemn her for her past.

Yes, the accusing voice in your mind may be right in some of the accusations but so were those who accused the adulterous woman. Jesus's response to you is the same; he does not write you off, he calls you to change. One voice wants to hold you in shame, and paralysed by your sin the other voice wants to free you from your past and set you on a path to God and blessing.

So if the voice of God isn't condemning you then who is? Once again Jesus invites us to understand who our real accuser is…in the book of Matthew chapter 13 Jesus tells a story. In the story he compares God's kingdom to a farmer (Jesus) who scattered seed (God's truth) to grow a crop (God's children).

Then he told them many things in parables, saying: "A farmer went out to sow his seed. As he was scattering the seed, some fell along the path, and the birds came and ate it up.

*Some fell on rocky places, where it did not have much soil.
It sprang up quickly, because the soil was shallow. But
when the sun came up, the plants were scorched, and they
withered because they had no root. Other seed fell among
thorns, which grew up and choked the plants.
Still other seed fell on good soil, where it produced a
crop—a hundred, sixty or thirty times what was sown.
Whoever has ears, let them hear (Matt 13:3-9, NIV).*
What does this all mean? Jesus explains its meaning…
*"Listen then to what the parable of the sower means:
When anyone hears the message about the kingdom and
does not understand it, **the evil one comes and snatches
away what was sown in their heart.** This is the seed sown
along the path. The seed falling on rocky ground refers to
someone who hears the word and at once receives it with
joy. But since they have no root, they last only a short time.
When trouble or persecution comes because of the word,
they quickly fall away.
The seed falling among the thorns refers to someone who
hears the word, but the worries of this life and the
deceitfulness of wealth choke the word, making it
unfruitful.
But the seed falling on good soil refers to someone who
hears the word and understands it. This is the one who
produces a crop, yielding a hundred, sixty or thirty times
what was sown."*

The true nature of the accuser in your life is a spiritual
force Jesus called the evil one, our enemy, he comes to kill
and destroy. It is this evil voice who stands on our
shoulder and whispers into our ear, 'You are not good
enough'. With his accusations he steals the truth from your
heart and over time you believe his accusations.

If you want to be free from the accusations of our enemy, then you need to let Jesus in.

Only Jesus can free you from the accuser's voice. I know for me it was the beginning of freedom.

The day I allowed Jesus's voice to drown out the accuser's voice I began to hear the truth…I was valuable enough for God, Jesus died for me, God wants to help me change my life from wrong to right. God's spirit began to heal my broken inner parts, heal my past hurts, helped me to forgive and set me free from the hate I bore to those who hurt me.

I'm still flawed in more ways than I want to admit and I still make choices that hurt me and others but now when the accuser's voice comes to me and says, 'See, you're not good enough, God doesn't love you', my response is, 'I won't listen to your lies because "God chooses me" because "God is good" even when I am not.

Chapter 4
Can I find healing?

With Jesus and coffee, I can do anything.
I pray you forgive my jest but sometimes this seems completely true in my life. What is true in my life is that if I start my day in my 'time with God' chair with a scrumptious hot flat white in my hand then there is nothing I cannot achieve, no problem I can't manage, no difficult person I can't humour or forgive. The opposite is equally true, if I do not start my day with Jesus and a coffee then difficult people get the better of me, my frustrations rob me of my joy and some days I finish wondering how I can do it all again tomorrow.

Now before I start a new religion based on the power of the flat white coffee I'm pretty sure it's the Jesus part that's more important. No, in fact it has nothing to do with coffee but for me they are a beautiful collaboration. I am grateful to the teaching of Bill Hybels on this subject and if you have the inclination I encourage you to find a book called, 'Simplify' which artfully unlocks the power of 'Time with God'. However, I hope that you will find the same simple truth in this chapter. We were never designed to 'Do life' alone.

Most of us are aware of this and gather some significant people to 'Do life' with - our wives/husbands, parents, children, friends and other significant people.

In my experience very few of us ever understand that we also need a relationship with the 'Living God' every day as well. Doing life without God is like driving a car without changing the oil.

Our jobs, friends, family, pleasures, holidays, all these things are like putting Gas in the car but without a regular supply of fresh oil the car will eventually break down and eventually be un-drivable.

Without Jesus in our lives the engine of our life eventually seizes and fails. For those who have never had this kind of relationship with God then you are about to discover a life-changing truth. We were designed to walk with God every day. It's in our DNA.

I love the second story of creation in Genesis. I love the imagery of Adam and Eve walking in the garden of Eden in the cool of the day. They didn't walk alone; they walked together and you are left with the impression that it was their habit to walk also with the Lord God Almighty. You are left with the sense that there was a fulfilment and peace in this until they disobeyed God's only law and ate of the tree of knowledge of good and evil. From that moment on it was no longer possible to walk with God in the garden. They were expelled to earth as we know it where God would no longer walk with them in peace because of their sin.

As we follow the stories in the Old Testament we see God continuing to walk with his people but it was always marred by sin and separation. This all changes when Jesus comes into the world. God made himself human in his Son, 'Jesus'. This is mystery too great for our minds to grasp but its implications for us as the descendants of Adam and Eve are enormous.

Jesus's death on the cross took upon himself our sin and destroyed the separation between us and God. Once again we are made friends of God and are able to walk again with our creator in peace. It's not the garden of Eden.

It's even better. It's 'Eternal life'. It's heaven, it's perfect peace.

This is a simplification of a very large and powerful story of God's walk with his children. So what does it mean for me? It means that with Jesus and coffee there is nothing we cannot do. When we believe in Jesus we do the only thing able to please God and reunite us to him.

In John chapter 6 people following Jesus asked him how they can please God, how they can know God? In verse 28,

'Then they said to him, *"What must we do, to be doing the works of God?" Jesus answered them, "This is the work of God, that you believe in him whom he has sent.'* (ESV)

A little a bit further into the conversation, '*Jesus said to them, "I am the bread of life; whoever comes to me shall not hunger, and whoever believes in me shall never thirst. But I said to you that you have seen me and yet do not believe.*
All that the Father gives me will come to me, and whoever comes to me I will never cast out. For I have come down from heaven, not to do my own will but the will of him who sent me. And this is the will of him who sent me, that I should lose nothing of all that he has given me, but raise it up on the last day.

For this is the will of my Father, that everyone who looks on the Son and believes in him should have eternal life, and I will raise him up on the last day.'

When we understand that it is God's plan to once again walk with us in perfect friendship through our relationship with his Son Jesus, we can start to climb those mountains in our life, tackle those difficult relationships, work toward the desires of our hearts, fulfil our life's calling.

Paul wrote in the letter to the church in Philippi in chapter 4 describing the many challenges he faced in his life's calling but in the face of them all he says in verse 13, 'I can do all things through him who strengthens me'(NRSV).

For Paul, with Jesus in his life he could face all the challenges with the knowledge that God was with him. This is a powerful belief and one that empowered his life. Paul's life continues to reverberate and influence the world in ways far greater than he could ever have imagined.

Okay, I want to take this powerful truth and make it a belief with legs. In my life this powerful belief takes shape in a very practical way every day when I sit in my 'time with God' chair with my coffee.

Oh I can hear the excuses already, 'I tried that once', 'I'm too busy', 'I have small children', 'I'm not a morning person' I'm sure there are even better ones than this. I confess that I was someone who used all these reasons at different stages in my life.

I would have to say if I could turn back the clock it's the first thing I would change. I would grab my past self and explain how powerful this simple belief is and how the day I chose it my life changed for the better.

I can explain how I find peace in my anxieties, healing for my hurts, confidence for my future, empowerment in my sense of calling, an all-conquering love, a port in the storms that sometimes rock my life. I'm not saying it's a cure for all my problems; I'm saying it's the living God walking with me in them. WOW, that still blows my mind, 'Thank you Jesus'. So this is what I do and I'd encourage you to follow or find a similar effective plan.

My Plan for walking with the Lord

Step 1: wake up at 6am (this does vary I must confess) and put on something warm.

Make my coffee.

Step 2: Sit in my designated prayer chair. 'I only sit in it to pray and think; this makes it special (it's blue)'.

Step 3: Close my eyes and calm my thoughts, silence my mind. (If I'm having trouble with this step because my mind is filled with problems or just racing, I stop and write them all down in my journal so I can deal with them later.

Step 4: Once my mind is clear I take 5 -10 minutes to pray, asking God to help me with my day and give to him my concerns and people I'm praying for. It's important in this step to thank God for the many blessings in your life. I try to be specific, for my children, wife, job etc. In my experience a 'thankful heart' is a happy heart.

Step 5: Open God's word. For me I follow a bit of an organic plan. I will pick a book in the Bible and work my way through it. I will also use my Anglican lectionary (a guide that runs you through the whole Bible every year). If you're someone who likes being systematic in things, then you might like to purchase a Bible reading plan or use a lectionary.

Personally I like to be a little more organic and sometimes I sense God leading me towards a particular book. With my preaching I like to keep the discipline of the lectionary, it prevents me from pushing my own agenda from the pulpit.

Step 6: I journal/pray/listen. The best way to explain this is that I'm actively seeking the voice of God. I actively ask God to speak to me through his word and prayer. I'm listening and keeping my mind focused on God's word. I write down in my journal what I feel God is saying to me and how it looks in my life.

The amount of time spent in each step varies and if my day is really busy I sometimes have a tendency to want to fast-track each step. I have learned however that the fast track is a mistake. This is not a time-based process, sometimes I'm done in 30 minutes, sometimes an hour, and in days I'm really troubled it can be more.

That's why I start early to give myself the space if I need it. I have learned that I am better off choosing a different time in my day than fast-tracking my time with God.

If we begin to see our time with God as a burden or obligation it has already lost its power to impact our lives. I program my day around the things that really matter, not what I need to get done.

Truth be told there is never a day when I get everything I need to do done. Consequently, I need to prioritise the relationships and tasks that have the greatest impact in living out my calling and vision for my life. I can really only understand this vision and calling if I allow myself to be directed by God each day.

This is an excerpt from my prayer/listening journal (the part of the bible reading which spoke to me in my words, not a translation) -

Romans 8:12-14 Put to death the deeds of the flesh
John 14:27 Peace I leave with you, my peace I give to you.
Do not let your heart be troubled nor let it be fearful.
I feel the Holy Spirit saying to me I need to bring my
physical desires into obedience to Christ. To live by his
spirit and Jesus peace will rest on me.

This very simple guidance from God reminded me of my need to live by his Spirit and not be a slave to my physical needs.

His peace and the power of his Spirit can give me strength to resist physical temptation in all its forms and seek his presence to fill my innermost needs.

This guidance from God spoke loudly to me that day as I had been eating poorly over the last couple of days. I had been dealing with some stressful encounters at work and I have a tendency to use food as a crutch to manage my stress. God reminded me that his Spirit and prayer are the healthy way to deal with my stress, not food. I thank God that he desires to walk with me in all my struggles.

Why 'Coffee and Jesus' is different to 'Duty and guilt'
For a long time, my walk with the lord was 'feast or famine'. I would go to church and hear an inspiring sermon on how I should read my bible and have a devoted time of prayer and for a couple of weeks I'd set my alarm, get up early and force myself to read the bible for 30 minutes and spend 30 in prayer. This was really good for me and I benefitted from it.

Ultimately my motivation was guilt and duty and slowly but surely I began to skip a day then a week and then my time with God was relegated to 'God I need help' prayers. Life would get busy and it didn't seem a priority and especially when life was good.

Then I'd be talking to a Christian friend about their devotional life and I'd feel guilty again and I set my alarm again and for two weeks I would walk with God and then again life would distract me again. Can you see the pattern? Now some would read this and wrongly say, 'I didn't love the Lord'. I did however, and my love for Jesus was constant although strained by sinfulness and the absence of intimacy with God.

I can testify that my belief in Jesus was unwavering but I kept dropping my cross (Matthew 16:24-26). I went to see a pastor once about my problem and his response only made me operate out of more guilt; he said, 'pray for discipline, develop a pattern, or follow a rule of life'.

This wasn't bad advice; it just didn't understand the root cause of my problem. There was an important reason why my attempts at discipline and following a rule of life weren't working. I was operating out of a self-limiting belief which prevented me finding the Joy in walking with the Lord that I have now.

I want to share with you a story I have permission to use from a Faithful pastor friend of mine. Fr Michael is a Priest in the Anglican Church who served for many years amongst the Torres Strait Islander people of Australia and he did so with great love and conviction. He shared with me that part of his faith tradition being Anglican was to do morning and evening prayer each day following a rule of life or liturgical pattern. He would as a discipline follow the liturgy, read the bible and pray according to the pattern set down.

This was a good discipline and acted as an anchor in his life and ministry but he hadn't realised there was something deeply meaningful missing from it. It was duty more than relationship; it was more obligation than it was intimate. The day it began to change was the day he heard the Rev'd Nicky Gumbel talk about his quiet time with God over a cup of tea. Fr Michael had seen this devotional time as a reverent, serious time, a sacrificial time. Something about having a cup of tea seemed almost a contradiction to this.

Either way Fr Michael was inspired by this story and began to have a cup of tea with his morning prayer. He shared that it brought an intimacy to what had been a duty, it brought a life-giving sense of connection to what had been a religious piety. For Fr Michael a humble cup of tea brought a new vision of time spent in Gods presence. Remember, Gods presence is a gift freely given through Jesus sacrifice. Gods presence is never earned by our sacrifices.

Chapter 5

My life as a Masterpiece

It's easy to forget that we are painted by a great master. Indeed, the greatest of the masters. We are created with a perfection that finds its fulfilment when we place ourselves completely in the master's hands. We can't see the master but we can see each brush stroke if we choose to. Even more so we, together with the master, shape the very work itself. So many of us fail to realise that the painting is in progress with every day of our lives. The painting can be aimless and even trivial or it can be glorious and inspirational.

I liken it to those finger paintings that I still have that my children made for me when they were little. I love them but sometimes I wasn't actually sure what they were picturing until they explained it.

Compare this to the last time you went to an art gallery or viewed an art collection. The detail, the creativity, the passion, the beauty. The choice is ours. Will our life be a finger-painting limiting the master to 3 water colours and stick people or will we allow the master the whole palette of colours and a glorious vision of love, relationships, meaning, purpose, healing and wholeness.

Even our brokenness and failures can be made beautiful if we allow the master to have these parts of our life.

It's probably helpful to tell you about my time with Josie.

Josie came from a dysfunctional home where she experienced systematic abuse over many years. Her self-esteem was terrible, and at age 19 she battled with an eating and anxiety disorder. Josie heard me speaking on this topic and felt deeply troubled by it. 'How could God turn my painting into something beautiful, my life is ugly and I am ugly'.

I confess my attempts to help her see what was possible were a failure. Josie couldn't see a future with any value and the hurt was deep. I lost touch with Josie for many years until recently we crossed paths. I found Josie married with two cute little kids. 'Wow' were the words I uttered, 'look at you'. Smiling from ear to ear she said, 'I found love'.

It seems God had taken the ugliness and the brokenness and turned it into something beautiful. Josie told me she still struggled with her anxiety disorder and had to work on her eating but Michael and the kids had helped her find real meaning and purpose in her life.

I asked her if she felt her canvas was looking more like a masterpiece now?

Josie felt it was still a work in progress but that the master was certainly using brighter colours now.

An important question to ask ourselves is, 'Do I believe my life is a collaboration'?

We live in an increasingly individualistic society where we are encouraged to 'get what we want', 'have our needs met', 'it's my right' and other such self-orientated ideas. This however flies in the face of 'God's vision for human beings'. We were created to live collaboratively.

My canvas begins blank and every relationship, experience of others and relationship to the creator forms the brush strokes and the picture created. In the very beginning of the Master's book 'the Bible' we are invited to grasp the collaborative masterpiece that is our lives.

'So God created humankind in his image, in the image of God he created them; male and female he created them'.

How is this a picture of a collaborative masterpiece? It's not. It's an answer to the 'why it's a collaborative masterpiece'. Our life is so precious to God because the canvas itself contains the image of God. To take this to its natural conclusion, God imparted something of himself into us. When God decided to create me he gave his own image to be the canvas. Pause to think on this for a moment. If you grasp it… it's breath-taking.

The second part of the passage is equally important. 'Male and female he created them'.

We need to understand ourselves as whole when the complementary nature of men and women are brought into relationship.

Whether that is a complementary relationship with a spouse, a parent, a significant friend or friends, sibling, or any mix of the above. When we seek to live without the complementary dynamic of male and female in our lives we are not able to exercise the fullness of our humanity.

So how do we live our life to be a masterpiece? We have our Canvas made in the image of God, we understand that we must embrace the collaborative nature of producing a great work particularly embracing the male/female dynamic. What next?

What any great painter will tell you - 'Inspiration'. We visualise what we want to create, inspired by 'meaning and purpose' formed by the fullness of each 'Season' in which we live. Yet still something is missing? Does the master stop at providing the Canvas? Of course not - our masterpiece requires the brilliance of a master's brush strokes. Here is where it gets really interesting. If we invite him to do so the master will take our hand in his and begin the brush stroke unique to us but with the wisdom and experience of a master supporting and guiding.

If you're struggling to follow this metaphor imagine a small child wanting to paint a house.

On their own the house would be rudimentary even if the child was visualising something grand. When a parent with a gift for painting sits with them and talks with them about their vision for a grand house the parent can guide the child's hands and vision to create something far more detailed and beautiful than the child could have created in their own right.

Paul's Choice

There is a powerful voice in the Christian Church who at one time oppressed and persecuted Christians before having a powerful experience of God and converting. Upon his conversion he became an outspoken leader and teacher in the Church. So influential was he at building new churches and growing the faith that he was arrested and imprisoned to silence him. At his arrest and imprisonment, he faced a new and harsh reality...he may never be released. Indeed, Christian tradition says Paul was beheaded by emperor Nero after a lengthy house arrest.

The importance of this story lies in the power of a single question, 'Was Paul more influential before or after his arrest?' The obvious answer would have been before.

He went from building churches and making converts to being a prisoner. Yet somewhat surprisingly it is his time in prison which has made him one of the most influential men in the history of the Christian church. How can this be? In his freedom he is commonly credited with starting around 14 churches which in and of itself is more than most pastors will ever do. However, it is when we understand that from prison he wrote four of the most influential letters to his churches.

In these letters are teachings which became part of the cornerstone teaching of the New Testament in the bible.

For nearly 2000 years, generation after generation of Christian people have deepened their knowledge of God and their relationship with Jesus through reading and studying Paul's teachings. The 14 churches he started taught to a few thousand the Joy of knowing Jesus but his writings have taught many millions.

So what is Paul's choice? Having been arrested he could have given in to despair, complained at God for doing this to him. He could have seen this as the end of his influence and indeed his life.

Instead he says in Philippians 1:12-13, '*…what has happened to me has really served to advance the gospel, so that it has become known throughout the whole imperial guard that my imprisonment is for Christ*'.

He also wrote in Ephesians 3:1-10, '*For this reason I, Paul, a prisoner for Christ Jesus on behalf of you gentiles…, to preach to the gentiles the unsearchable riches of Christ and to bring to light for everyone what is the plan of the mystery hidden for ages in God. (ESV)*

Rather than seeing his imprisonment as God-given punishment he saw it as divine providence and sought to embrace what God could achieve through his imprisonment. The key understanding here is nothing to do with his imprisonment and has everything to do with Paul's response to his circumstance.

I meet too many Christians who are either angry at God for their circumstances or are waiting for their circumstances to change before they take up God's call in their life. If Paul had been angry at God for his imprisonment he would never have been so influential in shaping the Christian world.

If Paul had waited till his circumstances had changed, he would never have served God and brought so much solace and insight to millions.

Paul's Inspiration -I'm not a Victim

How do you know you've fallen into the snare of the 'Victim mentality'?

You look at most of the people around you and think they have it better than you. You aspire to be like people who have more stuff than you, better job than you, happier family than you, better looking than you.

You constantly see the success of others as a threat to your own self-worth, usually unconsciously then acted out with criticism and negativity toward the other person's success. You constantly feel the need to defend yourself even when you know you are in the wrong or have stuffed up. It wasn't really your fault if someone else had been doing their job properly; it wouldn't have happened to you. These are just a few indicators and I'm sure you recognise these either in yourself or someone in your life.

I remember being derisively labelled as 'Moses' by one of my friends because they said my life was so 'Holy'. This judgement was based on the choices I made according to my faith. I was seen as a 'goodie goodie' because I would do the right thing rather than the popular thing. It was also laden with a victim mentality. My life of one wife, four healthy loving children, good job seemed all too perfect compared to their broken and messy life. Ironically if my friend had been a little more informed about the life of Moses they would have chosen a different measure.

Moses's life was hard and filled with mistakes and sometimes poor choices (I do identify with the mistakes and poor choices), however ultimately Moses was obedient to God and chose to live according to God's will.

I too seek to live in obedience to God's will and with the forgiveness gifted to me by Jesus and the work of God's Spirit in my life I am able to walk in his will.

However, my friend's judgement of me as 'Moses' came from their own victim mentality and had nothing to do with the messy reality of my life. All my friend could see was the blessings in my life, not the blessings in their own. The truth was that my friend's life was full of reasons for thankfulness; they just couldn't see them because they were so busy feeling victimised by what was missing or wrong rather than empowered by what was good and possible.

What is possible in your life?
If you know you have a tendency toward a victim mentality or perhaps you realise you've been waiting for things to improve before you act, then today is the day to change.

A habit I have taught myself and my children from a young age is to physically and verbally list my reasons to be thankful in life, the people I have to be thankful for, the humble gifts and talents I possess. When the kids were really young it would be at the dinner table and they would say, I'm thankful for Mummy and Daddy, my puppy, my full tummy and many other cute blessings.

As they grew older it would be for their friends, their successful exams and I hope they will be like me when in adulthood - thankful for their measure of health, their belonging to God, their call to serve and the gifts they have been given to use. If you had asked me five years ago if I would be the author of six books I would have chuckled because at the time I didn't think that was my gift or my calling.

But I would also have said, 'You never know what God can achieve through someone who believes it's possible'. In my Church we have a list of ten organisational cultures we strive to live out in our ministries. The one that has had the greatest impact on me is, 'I am a can-do person, experience is less important than the willingness to see new possibilities'.

For me I see a powerful God at work in a person who believes that 'God is able to do immeasurably more than all we ask or imagine' (Ephesians 2:20) and no surprises that this was Paul's teaching.

It begs the question, 'Why do so many of us fail to live up to our potential'?

There are a number of possibilities but I would like to focus in on one I see all too often, 'Guilt'.

Sometimes we are held back from believing God wants to do amazing things in our lives by our past and even the daily guilt trip.

Chapter 6

Guilt doesn't serve us well

I remember coming home one day after work and finding Michelle frazzled and emotional, worn out and at her wit's end with our four small children. I made a classic male mistake in that moment…I sat down. A clever male would recognise the signs, agitation, hair dishevelled, one word answers, messy kitchen and acted quickly. He would have run the bath, ordered her in, made a cup of tea and started cleaning the kitchen and making dinner.

The world would have been a better place in that moment and I would have been a hero. Anyway back to reality. *You come in and just sit down…you don't care about me at all…*you know the rest of this dialogue, you've been there.

Once the tears had stopped, I had apologised and made that cup of tea and the kids were in bed we talked about what had really happened. It wasn't really about me sitting down, it wasn't really about whether I cared, it was about guilt.

For many of us our emotions bubble over when we are out of our depth because we feel like failures.

Why is it that everyone else (these people don't exist by the way) can do this and I can't? Why do I feel this way? What am I doing wrong? The irony is that the powerful emotion behind our sense of failing is Guilt.

Somewhere in our conscience and even unconscious mind we harbour the belief that successful people, good mother/fathers can do this and so we feel guilt for the outburst and for the failure. Michelle felt guilty for not being on top of everything and then felt guilty for taking it out on me, then felt guilty for not trusting God more. Guilt can be suffocating.

If you're someone who lives with guilt you will know its power. Wikipedia says Guilt is 'a cognitive or an emotional experience that occurs when a person realises or believes - accurately or not - that he or she has compromised his or her own standards of conduct or has violated a moral standard, and bears significant responsibility for that violation. It is closely related to the concept of remorse'. Good job wiki but my translation is, 'I feel bad when I don't do what I think I should have'.

Ladies for many of you, your society, parents and even friends in your life (often quite unconsciously) have programmed you to operate in a constant state of guilt. The classic example is the modern phenomenon of the 'Superwomen' or 'Supermom'.

Able to raise children, work full-time, keep a perfectly clean house and a happy marriage all while looking gorgeous and well-groomed.

Pop culture rather pretentiously touts this as the pinnacle of the feminist achievement. Instead of a feminist success story I believe this is a false paradigm and although it looks like equality it is in fact a new kind of inequality.

A woman can feel programmed to feel guilty about not being with her children when she's out with her friends. Guilty when she's at home with her children when she hasn't been a very good friend. Guilty that she doesn't feel bad for not inviting her mother in-law for the kid's party but guilty for not being a better daughter-in-law. Guilty that she hasn't been more interested in the bedroom activities, guilty that she hasn't been eating right and exercising more, guilty that she hasn't been taking the kids to church regularly enough.

Guilty that she spends so much time at work or guilty that she doesn't work enough to help with the bills. I could spend the rest of this page on the things a woman can feel guilty about. Perhaps the greatest irony of all this is that you feel guilty for feeling guilty because you know how silly it is.

This is not to say that men are free from guilt and can be subject to conditioning as well but it is less about equality and performance and more about identity. A man can feel guilty if he's unemployed and unable to provide for his family, a man can feel guilty if he's been unfaithful to his wife.

A man can feel guilty when he claimed a birdie on the fourth hole when he knows he didn't count the duff shot in the rough (this is golf talk for those who think I just lost my mind).

A man can feel guilty for looking at pornography or cheating on his taxes and even for not helping out enough around the house. The difference is that a man will spend significantly less time feeling guilty and punishing himself for his failures.

A woman can spend her whole life immersed in life-destroying guilt if the light bulb moment doesn't come.

A man will go in and out, more out than in. These are generalisations and you may be one of the women who are largely untroubled by guilt or one of the men controlled by it. Either way if this isn't you I am pretty confident you know someone who is.

What's wrong with me? (guilt)
Playgroups and mothers' groups are for many parents a God-send and places of incredible nurture and belonging. However, for some parents like my friend Josie they are her worst nightmare.

In the first one she tried the women were all very well dressed with manicured lunches in perfect Tupperware containers for their children.

Josie said she felt like a hippo at a circus in her faded pink blouse and last year's fashion. No one said anything but their sideways glances and quiet conversations told her this wasn't for her. Josie left feeling guilty that she hadn't looked after herself well after the birth, and guilty for not being more organised and a better mother.

Undeterred she looked for something a little more low-key in another suburb and found one which looked more like her. She sighed with relief when she saw the casual clothes and imperfect food containers. 'Finally', she thought.

Until it came time for sharing. Josie discovered her child was the only one not sleeping through the night. Josie's child was the only one no longer breast feeding at 6 months, Josie's child was the only one not enrolled in a second language for babies' program. Josie left feeling guilty that she was not a better mother, with better knowledge.

Josie has given up on playgroups but not on having friends who are going through the same challenges.

Her final remark to me was, 'At least I don't feel so guilty now, there's no-one reminding me where I'm failing as a mother'.

How do I conquer guilt?

There are many self-help books out there and some cognitive behavioural therapists who might offer some helpful tools and changes in patterns of thinking and behaviour to deal with guilt. If you've already been there and tried that, then perhaps it's time to introduce a non-self-help process.

As a pastor in a growing church with young families I see the perils of operating in guilt on a daily basis. In fact, there are expressions of Christianity which actively encourage guilt as a motivator for faith and obedience.

It's at this point I think we need to delve into 'why' we experience guilt and whether it's an emotion God designed us to feel or an unhealthy departure from God's plan for us.

Our God-Given Conscience

When we follow the story of humanity's wrestle with God in the bible we discover that we are uniquely made in God's image. Designed to reflect his Glory and creativity and capable of Love. We also gain the knowledge of good and evil and the ability to choose between them. In the book of Deuteronomy, we hear God speaking to his people saying that from now on, 'I will write my law in your hearts'.

In the book of Romans 2:14-15, Paul speaks of people who do not believe in God, yet 'they show that what the Law requires is written on their hearts, to which their own conscience bears witness…'. We all have a 'God-given' conscience, an awareness of right and wrong that we are capable of listening to.

This is a healthy voice in our lives and can save us from making mistakes and guiding us into healthy life choices. The question is whether we are listening to this healthy voice in our lives or as we see in Paul's warning to young Timothy in chapter 4 we can 'sear our conscience like a hot iron'.

I remember as a child of 10 being offered a cup of coffee when I was staying at my friend's house. I had never tried it but it seemed a very adult thing to do and like most 10-year-olds I wanted to be seen as much older. Besides, if my friend was having it then I wanted to fit in and be seen as more adult-like. They said, 'Do you want one spoon of coffee or two'? I didn't know so I said with a great big smile, 'Two thanks'.

Then they asked, 'Do you want milk'? I didn't know, I had milk on my breakfast cereal and liked it so it had to be good in coffee as well, so I nodded my head very knowledgeably and said, 'Sure'. Then they said, 'Do you want one sugar or two'? I didn't know so I smiled as wide as possible and said, 'Two thanks'.

This adult concoction sure was complicated. Next thing I know there it was in front of me.

I didn't know what to do next so I copied my friend's father who took a great mouthful. Well my mouth was seared by the hottest thing it had ever known.

I did the only thing a very mature 10-year-old could do when his mouth is on fire, I spat it out all over my friend and fell backwards off the chair. Any delusions of grandeur I had at being a mature 10-year-old drinking coffee with my friend ended right there. I spent the rest of the night with ice in my mouth and begged them not to ring my parents and take me home. I had burned my tongue and mouth so badly that I seared my taste buds.

I couldn't taste much more for the next few days but thankfully my taste buds recovered, although to this day I'm very hesitant when I take my first sip.

This is much like our conscience, it speaks to us of those things that are rewarding and good for us and speaks to us of those things that can hurt and diminish us.

If we consistently ignore our God-given conscience and do what we know to be wrong over and over, it is like drinking a too-hot cup of coffee.

It burns our taste buds so we can no longer taste that which is good and that which is bad. If we ignore our conscience or allow others to override our conscience, then it will be burned away so that we no longer hear the voice of danger, and the voice of evil has no internal filter to stop it.

We saw this rather dramatically in World War 2 when normal everyday Germans allowed the propaganda of the Nazi party to sear their consciences to the point that they were capable of truly evil acts against their fellow human beings.

At the same time there were stories of everyday Germans who followed their conscience and saved lives sometimes at the expense of their own. We can externalise this to big examples like WW2 or we can acknowledge that every day our conscience is challenged and every day we must choose.

When I was a Uni student I would catch the train from home to Uni every day and like most Uni students I was constantly broke. (It had nothing to do with half-price jugs of beer on Thursday nights at the Regatta). At the age of 19 I had discovered God's interest in me and had made a commitment to follow Jesus.

This was such a joy and I was on cloud nine as I discovered just how much God cared about me and my insignificant life. Discovering at 19 that God has a plan for your life with meaning and hope is incredibly transforming. However, I also discovered my conscience had come alive again. Suddenly things I did on a daily basis without even a moment's thought became confronting and I was struggling with feelings of guilt about them.

One such change was the train ride to Uni and back. I, like many of my peers had developed the artful skill of avoiding paying the train fare. I could outrun and evade ticket collectors, jump barricades and turnstiles. This was an important skill and one I had considered morally acceptable because everyone did it so it must be right.

I became greatly conflicted by my competing voices over which was right. I shared my dilemma with my pastor who said, 'Sounds like your conscience is getting to you'. I had never heard this statement before but I sort of knew what a conscience was.

Thankfully in my new relationship with God I asked for help. I felt I heard a gentle voice in my heart say, 'What does your conscience tell you is right'? I was reading the bible regularly by this time and I knew that God prized honesty in his people. It became clear to me that evading my train fare was wrong and that just because others were not listening to their conscience didn't make it right.

From that day on I drank less beer and paid my train fare, which was my second lesson…the truth may set you free but it will often come at a cost. This was a truth that many Germans who listened to their conscience discovered.

What I am suggesting is that Guilt can be healthy if it is an emotional response to choices we are making which ignore our conscience. This guilt emotion is in response to our internal conflict.

It is healthy when we respond to the guilt feelings but listen to our conscience and make the necessary changes. Without these positive changes our guilt can become destructive and unhealthy, leading to a 'seared' conscience and emotional and physiological problem.

Chapter 7

What about my work/life balance?

When I read books or articles on managing our work/life balance they usually focus in on two things. One is achieving your goals and then effective time management. When I listen and watch the images our modern media projects from small and big screens we are encouraged to believe that we can 'have it all'. We are encouraged to believe that our success and happiness depends on our prosperity, attractiveness, influence and sex life. What I would like to draw our attention to is how powerful these ideas are. The reason why these ideas have so successfully entered and taken hold of our culture is that they appeal to our hunger. They also contain some truth. Have you ever heard the saying that 'a good lie must contain some truth'?

We all have different hungers but we can generalise them into needs for power, pleasure, prosperity, pain avoidance, fame, security and love. The ideas of goal setting, time management, you can have it all, success breeds happiness, are ideas that promise to deliver what we want.

Unfortunately, none of these ideas mentions the price we will pay to obtain them. Our goal-setting mentors tell us to be single-minded and focused.

Our time managers tell us it's about quality time not quantity, our social engineers on screen tell us happiness is a feeling we can obtain if we look right, dress right, have the right stuff. Our pleasure advocates tell us we need to manage our stress with better down-time with better toys, our relationships and sex lives should have more pleasure in them or they don't meet our needs. Our fame culture tells us that all fame is good and obtaining it gives you significance and success.

These are powerful motivators because they appeal to our most basic desires and wants. But are they completely 'truthful'?

When I talk to busy mothers what they most need is peace in the midst of what seems endless struggle. Most busy fathers need more down-time and family time. Most young adults need to know their life's purpose, and to find Mr. or Mrs. Right. Most young children need more time with Mum and Dad, more hugs and story time. Most grandparents need to spoil their grandkids and enjoy a quiet pace of life. Single people need more enriching relationships and joyful companionship.

I don't know if you noticed but there is a huge disconnect between what we as a modern society believe will bring happiness and what we actually need to be happy. When I ask most people what they need to be happy it usually revolves around having more of the 'stuff' we are fed in our modern culture.

When I ask them what actually makes them happy it's usually very different and centred on family, friends and health and enough money to do the simple things in life. So why this disconnect between what we 'want' and what we 'need'?

I'm going to talk more about identifying our needs versus wants but first I'd like to take us on a journey into the real cause of work-life imbalance.

First things first

Take a moment to write down the things that bring you peace, joy, love, hope, and faith. i.e. for me *my wife Michelle and children Tom, Emma, Harry and Bella bring me love and joy, my faith gives me hope in my struggles and my church and bible encourage me to be all that God destined for me.*

Peace comes when I put things in the right order, time with God, one heart with my wife, being the best father I can be every day, loving my flock. Laughing with my family and sharing our lives together, good food.

Your turn

Read back through your list and make sure it's not 'what you believe will make you happy' but rather 'what does make you happy'. I'll give you a clue: if it includes winning the lottery it's 'what you believe will make you happy'. If you were unable to write down what makes you happy don't be discouraged; this book can potentially help you most of all.

Did you notice that the things that make you happy didn't require you to be famous, to be rich, it wasn't about time management, it wasn't just about sex (it is sex with quality emotional connection)? For those who are single did you notice that quality time with friendships and family can bring love and joy and peace?

Did you notice that how big your house was or the type of car you drive didn't define your happiness? The house might need to be clean but not grand.

Did you notice the place of money in your list was only to allow you to spend time with family or meet the basic needs of your family happiness? Was God in the list?

There is a simple truth here. If we want to find a healthy work/life balance, we need to put first things first. If our work takes so much of our time and emotional energy that we are unable to live the life that is worth living, then something is wrong.

Have you started with the 'BUT' objections yet?

I have to work, I have bills, a mortgage, I need this job. 'YES' we need to work, we need good jobs and ambition is good. Is this the part where we talk about time management? Noooooooooo!!!!!!!!

It's about first things first!

I am privileged to do marriage counselling and in walking with struggling marriages I have learnt the power we have to 'choose' happiness or 'dysfunction'. It's the choices we make that decide whether our marriages are happy or miserable, our children grow to love us or walk away from us when they are old enough. These choices always centre around the place of work/family/money and God.

To help you understand what I'm talking about I want to share from my own life a pivotal moment in my marriage. I was working in a church which was growing and developing some great discipleship and becoming financially strong. This is a good place to be; most of the churches I work with constantly battle with financial challenges, and struggle with low levels of engagement.

However, it was a success very dependent on my working long hours and more importantly investing all my emotional strength.

At the same time, we had four children in the local private school and the financial pressures which come with this.

Michelle was offered a great job in the local hospital in senior management within her field of expertise. In some ways it was a dream job and it certainly solved all our financial problems. Michelle took the job and initially it presented some challenges around time management and drop off and pickup with the kids but we figured it out.

We had made the decision on the basis of what seemed logical to us and certainly ticked all the boxes of our modern culture. We had more money, Michelle had more power and influence, I had growing credibility in both the community and wider church for my success. Michelle was super mum and we were both success stories…or were we? Michelle and I began to have less time together, and less time with our children.

We didn't realise it at the time but one of our children was being badly bullied at school and his behaviour deteriorated and we had no idea why. I was so exhausted by my role that I was less engaged with my family, and even when I did have time with them I wasn't really present when I was with them. I'd talk about quality time not quantity time but looking back it was neither.

My children were having all the struggles kids have with friendships and study and neither of us were as available as our children needed because of our focus on work. I particularly had no time for friends and I slowly drifted away from any support network I had. I was gaining weight and not exercising.

There was less and less romance and less and less intimacy in our marriage. My time with God got thinner and thinner and less and less important, I was too busy running God's church to spend time with him.

I say all this now with the benefit of hindsight but at the time I was so focused on my goals that I couldn't see the cliff I was heading toward. Thankfully even though I didn't understand what was going wrong I knew something wasn't right and so did Michelle. I was so blinded by my 'wants' that I had lost sight of what was really important.

I had stopped putting 'first things first' and allowed the half-truths of prosperity and success to lead me away from the truly life-giving destiny God had gifted me. Michelle and I made a decision which I believed saved our son from a very destructive path, a decision that saved my health both physical and emotional; a decision which gave Michelle back her greatest calling and joy.

What was that decision? We put 'first things first'.

Jesus taught ...Therefore do not worry, saying, 'what will we drink?' or 'what will we wear?' For it is the gentiles who strive for all these things; and indeed your heavenly father knows that you need all these things.

But strive first for the kingdom of God and his righteousness, and all these things will be given to you as well. So do not worry about tomorrow, for tomorrow will bring worries of its own. Today's trouble is enough for today. Matthew 6:31-34

We sat down and prayed; we talked and talked and talked about what was really important for our marriage, what was really important for our children, what was really important for our calling to be children of God. It didn't take us long to realise we had to make major changes.

I finally got my priorities in the right order again - my relationship with God, my role as a husband, my role as a father then my role as a pastor. With both our sets of priorities back in order we began to see clearly that we needed to make changes.

If I wanted to continue being a pastor, I needed to hand over many tasks to trained and empowered members of the church. This would give me back some of my time and emotional energy.

I needed to be more available and present in my marriage and my role as a father. I needed to prioritise quantity and quality time. This meant letting go of some of my ambitions which were about my ego and sense of self-worth which were both misplaced.

Michelle felt she needed to work less and this was only possible if she resigned her position and went back to part-time work. This meant making significant changes to our lifestyle. With less money we decided we wanted our kids to stay in private education but didn't need our house.

Everyone told us not to, because it was a poor financial decision but we knew it was a good decision to allow Michelle more time to be a mother to our children.

Ultimately having made these choices we discovered the causes of our son's change in behaviour and realised in fact God was calling us to a whole new chapter in life. I took up a new posting and my son really blossomed in his new school.

In fact, all our children blossomed with a father and mother more available. It's true financially we struggle more because of our decision but when I think about what really makes me happy, it was the best decision Michelle and I ever made. I have no doubt that God will enable us to buy a house once again and that Michelle will take up full-time work again if that is her destiny.

For now, I am at peace knowing my marriage is strong and life-giving and my children are thriving and both Michelle and I have the time to enjoy this season in our life.

Okay now we are ready to talk about the difference between what we really need and what we think we want to be happy and find peace in our lives.

Need versus want

In life we need many things to live well. We need clean air, good nutritious food, loving relationships, gainful employment or financial capacity, clean water etc.

These are things that we can have in abundance or sparingly but we cannot live well without them.

There are also things we may want like prosperity, jet skis, more sexual intimacy, more friends, new fashions, better car but at the end of the day they don't really decide whether we are living well or not. They may bring greater pleasure or short term gain but they don't make as much impact on our lives as we might think.

The simple truth is that what we 'NEED' is critical to life and what we 'WANT' is not.

Now when we revisit our list of what makes us happy, how many of these things live in the NEED category and how many live in the WANT category? Usually if we live in the WANT category we will struggle to be happy in life.

There is nothing wrong with wanting a jet ski but if we believe it will make us happy we will quickly discover it is an empty promise.

I journey with people every day wanting to be happy but seeking it in things and places that they will never find it. Perhaps at this point it might be helpful to identify what you need to be happy i.e. for me *I need quality and quantity time with my wife and children, I need nutritious food, I need a job that not only pays my bills but makes the world a better place (for me that's helping people).*

I need enough money to put a roof over my family, food in their stomach and clothes on their backs.

I need quality time with my heavenly father and I need to listen to his voice and share my struggles. I need downtime that refreshes my mind and body, I need to exercise.

Chapter 8

Our God as the Wine Maker

A Red Wine Reading

A strange title I know but for those who appreciate a nice Red you might appreciate the metaphor. A good Red wine needs ageing/cellaring to reach its full potential. A good wine maker won't know a wine is ready for selling until he tastes it. The wine maker might suggest when he cellars a wine that the wine itself will tell him when it's ready. The wine maker must embrace the type of grape, the climate and soil it is grown in, then he must let the grape decide its own time for maturity. You might suggest the wine maker needs to embrace the wonderful mysteries each vintage holds.

This same principle can be said of our life experiences. I remember my first church as the Lead Pastor. Finally, after all my hard work, six years of study and assisting others, standing on the shoulders of giants. Now I was able to follow my sense of calling on my own terms according to my own pattern. Now before you go commenting on how unspiritual this sounds I, like most young pastors, was convinced I had all the answers.

Did I just make myself sound even less spiritual? What I mean is I was going to transform the Church!!!!!!

Okay it's true my motives weren't the best but we serve a God of infinite patience and he knew I meant well.

So back to the green pastor. My first Church was a beautiful old building steeped in many years of history and faithful servants. Did I mention that I actually had seven churches covering a territory of around 300km and a population of 7000 people?

I was based at the beautiful big church but a great deal of my ministry was to outlying areas and little churches we called 'God Boxes'. I would run church services on the properties of cattle Barons and small pastoralists. This was both an eye-opener and one of the most rewarding experiences of my short life. New to the church, no idea how to run church on a cattle station, not sure what they would make of me or my sermon let alone my music. But remember I was pretty convinced I had this.

Step 1: Find the property
Sounds simple, right? Have you ever tried navigating to a place where there are street signs about every 50km, T intersections with no sign posts, cattle grids in the middle of the road, kangaroos, mud and 'NO MOBILE RECEPTION' hence no GPS? Well you guessed it. I got horribly lost.

With wife and four little kids in tow (when are we there? 500 times), stress mounting, the 'why didn't you check before we left' question (seriously girls, really?). Screeeeeeech I slam on the brakes at the crest of a small hill, 'I've got mobile reception', so I call in the cavalry and one of the cattle Barons figures out where I am and drives out to meet me.

In my defence I wasn't far off but in this part of the world a little bit off can be a big deal. For a 3pm service for the surrounding properties with about 50 people waiting to meet the new guy I turned up at nearly 5pm. Head held low feeling pretty stupid and my guests reassure me it's no problem because these are all afternoon affairs. At the time I didn't know what this meant but I soon found out.

Step 2: Make a good first impression

It was probably already too late for this but what you have to understand about the Australian cattleman is that church is for women. His wife or mother makes him bath and put on his Sunday best and 'endure' church. This is not to suggest the Australian stockman isn't spiritual.

In fact, some were amongst the most deeply spiritual men I've ever met. But asking them to sit still in a formal setting isn't how they commune with God. Anyway back to my embarrassing little story.

I greet everyone and introduce myself and family then pull out my guitar and accompanied by my vocally talented wife we lead everyone in worship.

I was impressed by how energetically they joined in and thought, this is starting well. The men particularly seemed in good spirits in fact slightly too good a spirits. It wasn't until I got to my sermon that I realised one of the realities of my new flock. If you start church late they start drinking early.

Step 3: Preach a good sermon

You could say my sermon was interactive, rigorous, filled with robust conversation. Put simply it was like a comedy festival.

A couple of young barons were having a laugh at my analogy so I thought I'll counter with one of my favourite jokes guaranteed to get the audience back. This turned out to be another mistake as another responded with a better joke. Just when I though it couldn't get worse, one inebriated fellow dozed off and fell off his chair to raucous laughter and the chastisement of his wife.

The kids down the front were bored, the wives were agitated by the behaviour of their husbands and the men red-faced either from too much beer or trying so hard not to laugh. I needed a rock to crawl under. The one thing we all had in common was that we all wanted this Shakespearian tragedy to end so we could have dinner together.

Step 4: Try to sound intelligent chatting with the Men
So the service has ended and we all survived. Now comes the awkward, 'Our wives told us we need to be nice to the new minister' conversations. Now thankfully I had done my homework for this part of the Shakespearian tragedy.

I had researched cattle breeds and weather patterns, studied up on wheat cropping in western Queensland, after all I was a trained scientist. Some of the men engaged me in conversation about where I come from and how I'm finding the bush.
I'm positive and energetic and decide it's time to show the men I can play in their playground. So I start asking them about the breeds of cattle they run. Then I realise there was a breed they hadn't mentioned so I thought, 'Excellent, here's my moment to shine'. So I say, 'On my way here I saw some 'Desert Masters'. Are they common here?'
Stunned and awkward silence descends; the men share a knowing glance and a few wry smiles then one of the older (highly respected) cattlemen says, 'Stuart, do you mean 'Drought Masters'?' I needed that rock to crawl under again. I knew it was Drought Master but well arghhhhhhhhh.
Kind of means the same thing but to this day when I see these men some of whom remain good friends after many years they still remind me of this most embarrassing gaff.

Looking back, it was hilarious but at the time I wasn't laughing.

Step: 5 The Red Wine principle

This was not my finest hour but it's these experiences that either heighten our flavour or destroy it. These experiences can, like a good red, create a fragrance, a bouquet, which is far more enjoyable for those in our lives who receive our best and our worst.

For me as a pastor I find encouragement in Paul's words in 2 Corinthians 2:14,' *...but thanks be to God, who always leads us as captives in Christ's triumphal procession and uses us to spread the aroma of the knowledge of him everywhere' (NIV)*. God chooses us to spread Jesus's aroma to our friends and family, colleagues and strangers if we will but follow his procession.

Here are the things this day taught me. Trust not in my own strength or understanding but approach all ministry with a 'confident humility', Humility being the need for God in every part of our lives and Confidence in his desire to shine in and through us to his Glory, not ours. Always insist church happens before supper and be on time.

Be authentic in life and faith. Most of us smell fake in someone immediately and those who don't will eventually.

Now when I walk into a new place amongst strange people I walk in not as 'Stuart the gifted and overly confident pastor' but 'Stuart humbled and confident in God's choice to use me here in this moment'.

I would love to be able to say that this transformation was immediate but in reality I think it was many years of God's patient ministry to me through his people and his direct and breath-taking grace.

Like a good red wine my time in the Australian Outback with God's people and God's Grace cellared and rested my overpowering/overconfident tannins and acidic arrogance. Okay and yes I'm still very fruity but in a more enjoyable way (or so my friends tell me).

This is not to say that I think I've arrived. I haven't. However, I've embraced my life as a good red wine. My experience, successes, failures, times of effort and times of rest all reside in God's perfect timing as a wine maker. I have embraced the wine maker's efforts to make me aromatic and flavoursome by conforming to the likeness of Christ.

The best news of all is that our God is the perfect winemaker. He can take rubbish grapes in rubbish soil in a rubbish climate and make a 'Grange Hermitage' or a 'Chateau Lafite'.

When the Angels sing

I've often thought of life as a little like an orchestra. For our lives to make truly beautiful music we need others. Our families, our friends, collages and sometimes even strangers play their part in the orchestra of our lives.

Perhaps the part I love to ponder most is, 'Who is writing the symphony and who is writing the Opus'? The same is true in a pop group or hipster pack - who is writing the lyrics and the melody? Where is God in this orchestra or group? For me I find God increasingly in the lyrics and the melody; he writes my symphony and aids me as I ponder my opus. Let me put this into context. Most churches use music whether it's rock and roll, screamo, or Hymn music. Ask any Pastor and they will tell you that the most difficult team they manage is the musicians and singers/choir.

Now if this is you don't get pouty and indignant just yet, because it's also the most influential and important team for good and bad; just let me explain. Some years ago I was asked to conduct the Funeral of a well-known local identity and I knew it was going to be a big funeral. I knew the church would be full and that in some ways we would be on show for many non-church goers. I wanted to make a good impression so it was with some concern that a member of the deceased family asked to do a solo.

Now when it comes to funerals you tend to agree to most of the family's wishes. It's a time of great grief and you want it to be a place of healing and hope.

The problem is that I had heard this person sing before and to put it mildly it was …uncomfortable. How was I going to manage this disturbing piece of news? I consulted widely on this dilemma and thankfully a wiser soul than me recommended that, given the high emotion of the funeral, the family member had best use a choir and only do a part solo. Phew!! This was the answer I needed and with much prayer they agreed.

Catastrophe averted, or so I thought. Come the big day the Church was indeed full and the service was going well and now came the moment of truth. The choir began its sweet melody and like an angry mother-in-law at a wedding the soloist came in.

There aren't words to describe the horrors of the high notes and the lamentations in my heart in the low notes.

It was so 'uncomfortable' that the choir stopped because they could no longer find the note and the keyboardist fell behind as the soloist blazed a trail. It was so uncomfortable that I hid my face behind the service booklet so that no one could see my nervous laughter.

After the funeral I was stunned to hear people congratulating the soloist. I asked one of them, 'Did you really think it was good?'

He said, 'No, it was truly awful but she asked me what I thought and I was too embarrassed to tell her the truth'. It was this experience that taught me the meaning of Romans 12:3,

'For by the grace given me I say to every one of you: Do not think of yourself more highly than you ought, but rather think of yourself with sober judgment, in accordance with the faith God has distributed to each of you.' (NIV).

I suspect the soloist has had people over many years saying the same things, not wanting to offend. Sadly, if someone had really loved her (including me) we should have told the soloist before that it was a mistake.

This funeral has remained in my folklore as one of the world's most 'uncomfortable' funeral experiences. My point is this... the music designed to uplift and bring hope turned difficult for all who endured it.

So my question is...Is your life a sweet melody co-authored by a genius with a choir of angels? Or are you doing a solo act and still wondering why it's not working and no-one else wants to sing with you?

Chapter 9

Self-Sabotage

Why is it that on some days I feel unstoppable and why circumstances seem easily managed and I can find the positive in almost any situation? Why then a few days later do I feel derailed by the simplest things? Why does everything seem too hard and I just want to give up and get a different Job or different friends? What's happening in my life that I can swing from high to low? Is it my hormones? My diet? My circumstances? The cycle of the moon? Take a look through the self-help section of any bookstore and you'll find a book with an explanation and a guaranteed cure.

I'm actually not being cynical but truthful. The question I started to ask myself was, 'Am I the only one who feels this way, swings like this?' I posed this question to a well-meaning friend who suggested, 'It sounds bi-polar'. Needless to say this was unhelpful given that sufferers of bi-polar disorder experience dramatic swings outside their control and require medical attention. My response was, 'So anyone who has mood swings has bi-polar?

I'd love you to suggest this to your wife at that challenging time of the month'. Needless to say, my friend went quiet.

No this was not the symptoms of bi-polar disorder, in fact when I approached most people with this question their response was 'Duh, of course' (it seems I'm slow on the uptake). It did however lead me to a more important question, 'Do I have triggers in my life that cause the swings?' Equally, 'When I get into a 'funk' are there ways to turn it around quickly?' I wondered why some of the people in my life seemed to bounce back from disappointment or hurt faster than others.

Why grief destroyed some people while others seemed to rebuild in a healthy way? Why some people used healthy strategies to manage stress while others used self-destructive behaviours to manage stress.

Ask any psychologist, psychotherapist or psychiatrist and they will say there is no simple answer and every individual is different. Some would want to explore your formation from childhood; others would want to diagnose a pathology or disorder; others would talk about genetic or hormonal causes; some might want to look at your lifestyle and diet.

There is good science behind many of these approaches and for some of us good responses to treatment.

I would like to propose an additional possibility that 'what we believe' and how we act on these 'beliefs' become powerful forces for healthy responses to normal swings and changes in our lives. When I feel sad my beliefs can empower me or sabotage me.

When I'm anxious or fearful, what I believe can empower a healthy response or push me further into a downward spiral. In fact, if we develop a strong enough sense of intentional 'belief' in our life we can prevent many of our downward spirals, or at least shorten their length.

The power of what we 'Believe'

One of the hardest lessons I've learnt in life is that no matter what others may say about me or think of me it is what I think and believe about myself that has the greatest impact on my life. As a Christian what I believe about myself consciously is what Jesus tells me is true. I am a child of God, an inheritor of God's kingdom, I am forgiven and made whole, a new creation, I am loved and called to be a disciple. I can do all things through Christ who strengthens me.

No other person has power over me unless I allow them to have it. Growing up in my family, as in most households, name-calling is fairly standard amongst siblings.

My mother's response to our cries of, 'He called me ...' was, 'Sticks and stones may break my bones but names will never hurt me'.

To be really honest I think this is an ordinary piece of advice (sorry Mum, not that I'm a perfect parent either), because it's not true.

When I think back on it the emotional critics were more harmful than the physical from my siblings. It may be true that name calling won't break your bones but the emotional grenades thrown at you can create wounds and leave scars.

Read any good leadership book or life coaching manual and they will tell you that we don't often have control over what is done to us but we have complete control over how we react to it. When someone seeks to provoke a response from me it is up to me whether I give them what they want or what is in my best interest. As an employer I'm often looking to see how staff respond to correction and direction.

A mature person receives direction and correction if it is in their best interest to. If the correction or direction is inaccurate a mature person may ask for clarification and even disagree but ultimately make a decision based on their best interest to either receive it or find another job.

A self-sabotaging person will reject and fight against direction or correction even at the cost of their position, even if they know they are wrong. Why?

Often it is because their sense of self-worth was challenged or their upbringing or modelling was to fight against authority.

However, in my experience these overt forms of self-sabotage are far less common than the unconscious or more common forms of debilitating self-sabotage.

Jason

Jason was a nice young guy with a friendly disposition but seemed to flit from job to job, relationship to relationship and seemed unsettled. He was good looking, healthy and on the outside seemed like he had it together. When Jason came to see me he complained of being hard done by, 'Why was God doing this to me, why can't I get a decent boss? Why can't I find the right women?'.

To be really clear I was more than a little annoyed by Jason because I'd met some of these women and they were gorgeous and kind and the jobs were good. So it took a lot of self-discipline to sit and listen to his complaints. As Jason talked it became clear that he had a pattern of self-sabotage.

Whenever he had a good job he would allow a sense of entitlement to slowly erode his enjoyment in the role ultimately leading to frustration and becoming combative with his boss. Likewise, with his lady friends after some time he increased his demands on them because of what he felt he deserved in the relationship. This led to a sense of growing disappointment in the relationship.

Jason's immaturity was causing him to self-sabotage his life. I began by asking Jason to articulate what he wanted in his ideal girlfriend and ideal job/boss.

Let's just say that his expectations of a girlfriend were something like a porn-queen mixed with the best qualities of his mother, and a boss reminiscent of the fairy Godmother meets Stan the butler. His expectations were never going to be met.

When I held this mirror up to him he fought against it claiming his friends had found them. 'W*hich ones, I'll call them?'*.

I encouraged Jason to talk to his friends about the reality of their lives. What he discovered made him realise he had unrealistic expectations. In fact, he discovered his friends had been pretty annoyed at the way he had walked all over some great jobs and women they'd have died to have.

The simple truth was Jason had made his life about Jason which leaves little room for anybody else's need to be met. The consequences were self-sabotage. I then asked Jason to count the cost to his future if he didn't change his expectations of a relationship and of a job/boss. Jason became aware that the consequences of his false expectations were long-term unemployment and a single life.

There was still some important work for Jason to do in understanding 'why' he had false expectations.

Jason needed to understand that he was substituting short term pleasure in place of long term loving relationships. That expediency and the avoidance of pain in his working life were causing him to project his unhappiness onto his boss and job. Jason knew what he needed to do now but could he?

Jason's story leads us into an important question…Why is it that we know what we should do yet still we don't do it? We know we are trying to lose weight but the siren song of that Jam donut is just too powerful.

Paul famously wrote in the book of Romans chapter 7 verse 15, '*I do not understand what I do. For what I want to do I do not do, but what I hate I do*. (NIV)

I know if I go for that run I will be fitter and healthier and feel good about myself but it's too much effort. I know I should go to that work party; it would be good for my career to network but I hate those parties. I know I don't really need that dress and my credit card is hurting but it feels so good to buy it. Why do we self-sabotage? The answer is simple really. We don't like pain or stress or anxiety or depression or anything that costs us too much personal sacrifice, devotion or effort.

Being trained as a scientist I can tell you that the laws that govern the flow of energy in the universe tell us that everything wants to get to a state of least energy.

When we are running, after a while our body's natural tendency is a desperate need to lie down. When we've had a long day at work we are desperate to get home and we are faced with the choices of a slow time-consuming cooked meal or a stop for fast-food. Our natural tendency is fast food.

Now I know some of you are saying, 'No no no, I love my work' or 'I love to cook dinner', or 'I enjoy running'. Other than the slap that half the world's population want to give you right now, you are doing something that is either part of a survival mechanism or unique to human beings. We are governed by the laws of thermodynamics but we are able use them to achieve our goals as well.

But going back to the original point I was making, 'Why don't we do the things we know we ought to do?' I enjoy reading the stories of successful people in all endeavours because they have a common theme.

People who achieve great things all pushed into pain, discomfort, faced their fears and anxieties, were devoted to their goals.

These people were all willing to sacrifice short term pleasure and comfort, embrace short term pain, anxiety and sufferings because they were focused on the long term goal. Their hunger for their long term ambition far outweighed their desire for comfort and pleasure.

When you take this same idea away from the great people and take it into the everyday lives of you and me it looks like this...I don't like the discomfort and the pain of running but I'm so desperate to be fit and healthy to run that half-marathon that I will embrace that discomfort, I welcome the pain.

Perhaps its...yes the siren song of that donut is powerful and it will bring me great pleasure but a greater pleasure will be mine when I can fit into that dress again. I hope my point is now clear. Yes, the laws of thermodynamics are pushing you toward a state of least energy but you can choose to stay in a state of high energy (well into old age) if you are willing to choose it.

Self-sabotage is real and most of us engage in it on and off but if we can see it for what it really is, 'The pursuit of short term pleasure and avoidance of pain', then we can start to create a new sets of beliefs about our present and our future. I am going to lose weight because I'm willing to embrace the pain of my anxiety instead of stuffing my face with a donut to dull the pain.

I am going to go to that work party and network because my desire to rise through the ranks is greater than my desire to lounge on the couch or avoid the uncomfortable small talk. I'm going to put in that overtime because I really want that promotion even though I'm tired. I'm going to spend time listening to my children even though it costs me my downtime because I really want to invest in my children's future.

In essence self-sabotage is a failure to identify who you really want to be or what you want out of your life. You do not become who you want to be because you never set goals to achieve it, you never sat down and worked out what the price would be.

In the gospel of Luke chapter 14 versus 27 to 33 Jesus taught his disciples that if they want to achieve what God had called them to achieve then they needed to figure out what it would cost them to do it.

He used the example of a builder who wanted to build a tower. If the builder doesn't sit down and make plans and goals and count the cost, then he would build the foundation but not have the money or skill to finish it. Then he would be ridiculed as a failure.

Jesus then used the example of a king at war against a mightier army. Without wise counsel and planning, without counting the cost of going up against a vastly superior army he risked failure and destruction. Instead he is better off seeking peace because he'd counted the cost and knows he cannot win. Jesus finishes the teaching with an incredibly confronting truth.

He says, 'None can become my disciple if you do not give up all your possessions' (NRSV).

Now if you are like me and you own a house and other possessions you might be thinking, 'Does he really mean I can't live out my Christian calling to be a disciple unless I'm willing to sell everything I possess?' Yes, that's exactly what he means. God knows we need a roof over our heads and clothes on our back and food in our bellies so why would we doubt his provision of these things. The real truth is that if we were asked to sell our house to serve God, would we? When we decide we will give all we have we discover he gives it all back.

God doesn't need your house but he does want your heart and if we cannot put God ahead of our thirst for possessions then we won't choose to serve him.

If we are willing to count the cost of being a disciple, then Jesus will give us the anointing of his Holy Spirit to do that which we feel called to do. Whether you're an engineer or a hair dresser God has a calling and a ministry for you but we must be willing to count the cost.

Perhaps running a hairdressing salon where your Christian values are clearly articulated might cost you some customers or the tax agent who refuses to lodge false claims.

If we are ambitious for the things God values and are willing to count the cost of what it will take to get there, then there is nothing we cannot achieve according to God's purpose. History is littered with Christians who achieved great things because they counted the cost and knew how to avoid self-sabotage. When we decide to live our lives according to God's plan for us then we can count the cost and avoid self-sabotaging our calling.

What I believe?

This leads into one of the most important conversations in this whole book. What do you believe? As part of this chapter I've included an opportunity to write down what you believe. We are going to focus on specific areas. Remember with all these areas' you should find positive and negative statements so write them all down.

What you believe about God - be specific, not just 'I think' statements but 'I feel' statements. I feel I'm not good enough for God to use me, I believe I don't have any gifts or abilities to offer, I believe I don't know the bible well enough to talk to people about my faith. I believe God accepts me just the way I am; I feel Jesus is with me in my darkest times. I believe that no matter how sinful my life is, God's love is always reaching out to me.

I feel God gives me hope for my life, I feel my life choices make me a hypocrite - I could never belong to a church again. I feel hurt by the actions of Christians and they are all hypocrites, I don't want to be part of a church.

This is not an exercise in reciting scripture. Sometimes what we believe is actually in contradiction to what we know in scripture.

For example, Margery a long term Christian insisted that her ashes be buried in a box not scattered when she died because she believed it was important that her kids could come and visit her, not visit everyone scattered with her.

Scripture teaches that Margery is not dead but alive in Christ and awaiting the return of Jesus and will receive her new body. Margery's response was, 'I know that's what the bible says but I want my kids to know exactly where I am and not scattered with everybody else'. What Margery believed was in contradiction to scripture, not because she was disobedient or ignorant but because her belief was feeling-centred. She couldn't articulate what she felt but she believed it deeply. What we believe about God, especially if it's different to God's word will have a huge impact on our lives.

For example, Ralph wrote, *'I believe God loves me, I believe Jesus died for me, I believe I'm sinful in God's eyes but his grace is sufficient for me. I believe God wants me to get my act together, I believe my relationship with my girlfriend displeases God.*
I believe I'm not following God's call on my life. I believe I want to follow God's plan for my life.

Your Turn
What I believe about God - feeling and thinking beliefs…

2)**What we believe about ourselves** - again be specific. What do you think of yourself? Are you a good person, bad person, gifted, lacking gifts, easy to love, difficult to love, smart, a bit slow, happy, sad, anxious, depressed, optimistic, pessimistic? Statements like - I'm fat and unattractive, I'm too old to be of any use, this is just me and I can't change.
Feeling statements like - I feel lonely, I feel no one likes me, I feel I've got a lot to offer, I feel I'm caring of others, I'm not confident with people, I'm not a leader, I believe I'm a good guitar player.
For example, Ralph wrote, 'I'm difficult to love, I don't let people in to know me because I don't feel people really care about me. I've got a lot to offer but feel overlooked. I'm really good at sport and am quite intelligent. I believe I inspire people as a coach.
I am…

3) What I believe about change - again be specific. What do you believe is possible, what do you believe about creating new habits, what do you believe about past efforts to change, what do you believe would make change possible? Your belief about how change makes you feel, your feelings about past failures, your feelings about times you were successful in change.

For example, Ralph wrote -*I believe I would like to change some things about myself, I believe that past failures have made me doubt it's possible. I believe this is how God made me so maybe it doesn't need changing.*

I believe....

4) What I believe about my future - again be specific. I believe that if I don't lose weight I'll get diabetes, I believe I will have children, I believe I will have a husband, I believe I will be lonely, I believe I will be wealthy/poor, I feel God doesn't care about my future, I feel anxious and unsure about my future, I don't believe my husband/wife will still be with me, I believe there are good things in my future, I just want my future to hurry up.

For example, Ralph said - *I believe I will be married with three kids, I believe I will have a house, I believe I will be healthy and fit, I believe my future job is uncertain and I feel I don't I know what I want to do.*

I hope you have taken the time to do this exercise. I can't understate how important this exercise is to the value that the rest of this book can bring to your life.

Self-Limiting Beliefs Transformed

The point of the 'belief exercise' is to try to articulate what you really think/feel about your relationship with God, your relationship with your own soul, your understanding of your own capacity to change and what might be possible for your future. If we really engage with this exercise even the most self-aware will discover some beliefs that they hadn't realised were operating under the surface.

If you read through your beliefs and don't find anything new I'd encourage you to think deeper and feel your way into some of the more uncomfortable places in your heart.

What we need to do now is grab a highlighter pen or a pen of a different colour and highlight or underline under each heading belief statements that actually hold you down, hold you back, make you feel sad, or bad about yourself, your relationship with God, undermine your capacity to change and limit your future. You may think they are true but they still hold you back from being who you would like to be or who you are called by God to be.

These underlined or highlighted statements are beliefs that self-limit. Sometimes these statements might be the voice of someone in our life, maybe a parent or friend, an experience in the past. It doesn't matter where these beliefs come from; what matters is that you continue to believe they are true and they are holding you down.

Now I want us to go even further and circle one or two of these beliefs that are having the most destructive or limiting effect in your life. Maybe they make you the saddest, or cause you the most self-doubt. When you think about these beliefs ask yourself, 'What would my life be like if they were not true or better still not there?'

Take the time to write down how these key self-limiting beliefs are holding you back i.e. Ralph's self -limiting belief - *I'm hard to love*…means that I don't let people in, it means I have trouble making friends, it means I'm overly self-conscious about what I say or do when others are around. It means I avoid social interaction and gain very little soul-sustaining interaction with others.

What would my life be like if this wasn't true and that I was easy to love? It would mean I would let people into my life more, I'd probably have more friends. I'd probably feel less self-conscious and better about myself. I'd probably be more inclined to want to attend social functions and meet new people.

Take a few minutes to do this exercise.

My one or two key self-limiting beliefs and how they impact my life.

Inviting God's Spirit to transform your self-limiting beliefs

Having done the work of identifying the key self-limiting beliefs, you have to ask yourself the question...are they true? Our first response is probably, 'Yes', but I would encourage you to dig a little deeper. In talking to Ralph about his belief that he was difficult to love he had based it on experiences of the past. He had often found it difficult to maintain friendships and found himself uncomfortable in social settings. He had been rejected in a few relationships with the opposite sex and had also grown up in a home where friends were discouraged because they might challenge the loyalty of family or get in the way of family priorities.

On top of this he had felt let down by people whom he thought loved him and started to believe that people didn't really care about him so when they asked how he was he would fob them off. He stopped letting people in to prevent them from hurting him or disappointing him.

In talking to Ralph I explained that these were all fairly normal human experiences. All human relationships will disappoint or hurt us at some point, the real test of a relationship is whether we are willing to forgive and push past the hurt because we really want this relationship.

I also explained that, just because someone is more interested in themselves or even others around them doesn't mean their inquiry into your life is insincere.

As a rule, I choose to believe that everyone who asks me 'cares' whether they do or not, so that I don't become cynical or isolated. I also explained that most people are a little uncomfortable in a social setting especially if they don't know many people.

Remember we are all in the same boat so put yourself out there. You will be loved for it most of the time. All of us have people in our lives who just seem to be really good at socially connecting and mingling even with strangers. Usually these people have something in common and it's not that they are extroverts, it's usually because they've decided to be okay in their own skin and to make the most of the situation. They choose to find Joy in meeting new people and choose to enjoy themselves.

Even with my limited involvement with Ralph as his Pastor in both Church and social settings I was confident to say that he was easy to love.

To demonstrate to Ralph that what he considered 'truth' may not have been, he agreed to allow me to do a confidential survey of some of his friends. The feedback suggested he had his quirks but was loveable.

The interesting thing was that his friends said the hardest part about him to love was his tendency to be aloof. Can you see the vicious circle here? The more Ralph believed he was hard to love the more aloof he became, and the more aloof he became the harder he was to love?

Even in my own experience I am by nature an introvert but have learned in recent years to give myself to social occasions (which for me is every day) and believe that I am worth knowing and what I have to say is interesting (even if it's not).

I was able to turn my introverted belief from self-limiting to self-empowering by believing a 'new truth', one which turned around to be liberating for me. Besides this, I remind myself every day that, *'I'm made in the image of God'* and *'I can do all things through Christ who strengthens me'*.

So this is the moment you can make the most dramatic change to your life. Take those same one or two self-limiting beliefs and decide to believe the opposite. I'm not talking about denial.

We've all watched those episodes of 'American Idol' where people audition, believing they have amazing voices when in fact they sound like someone is murdering the neighbour's cat. No, I'm not asking you to believe something that is untrue. I'm asking you to turn, 'I'm difficult to love' to 'I'm easy to love' because what needs to change is your belief in what's possible. Is it possible for Ralph to be easier to love?

Yes, he simply needs to believe it's possible, and he will become more open and available to people in his life. Once he believes he is loveable he won't feel as awkward in a social setting; he won't choose to be so aloof with his friends. He can turn his vicious circle into a transforming and empowering new reality.

I am not espousing a tried and true self-help cliché. I'm talking about living God's promise in our lives. God can heal our brokenness; God can give us the strength to forgive those who hurt us.

Paul writes in the second letter to the church in Corinth chapter 5 verse 17, '*Therefore if anyone is in Christ, the new creation has come: The old has gone, the new is here!*' We are never trapped in old paradigms when we walk with Jesus. We are changeable, we are called to transformation into Christ's image, we are called to wholeness in God.

Are you ready to change your self-limiting beliefs? Are you ready to write a 'new truth' into your life? Take those original one or two self-limiting beliefs and change them into the opposite. Go for it.

God's Empowering Beliefs

We need to turn our attention to our empowering beliefs. Under each heading, highlight or underline the empowering beliefs. Beliefs that are most uplifting, energising, make you feel good about your relationship with God and with yourself. Which beliefs encourage you that change is possible, that my future can be bright and rewarding? Now circle one or two that have the most energising and positive effect on your life - beliefs that have the greatest potential to give you a future filled with hope and meaning in your relationship with God and yourself.

If you failed to identify any positives, I encourage you to go back a step and look for some. They are sure to be there if you think long enough.

When you think about these beliefs ask yourself, 'What would my life be like if I focused in on and celebrated these positive and life-affirming beliefs or what if I made them the centre of my life rather than the negative ones?'

Take the time to write down how these key self-empowering beliefs are holding you back i.e. *Ralphs self - empowering belief - I inspire people as a coach*...if this were at the centre of how I see myself in my workplace then I would probably become even more inspiring. I'd probably be even more intentional in empowering my teams to believe they can do it, that they can win.

I think more people would want to join my teams and I'd probably get paid more for what I do.

Take a few minutes to do this exercise.

My one or two key self-empowering beliefs and how they impact my life...

Imagine now if you made these key empowering beliefs the focus for your future. Do you think you are willing to believe them strongly enough for them to bring transformation in your life?

It is my experience in over 20 years of counselling that most people allow their self-limiting beliefs to guide them and their most powerful beliefs become subordinate to them. I meet so many Christians who even though they believe that God is with them, they allow the belief that they are not good enough to direct their life.

Imagine you lived a life where the knowledge that,

'For I know the plans I have for you' declares the Lord, *'plans to prosper you and not to harm you, plans to give you hope and a future'* (Jeremiah 29:11 NIV). Or the belief, *'and we know that in all things God works for the good of those who love him, who have been called according to his purpose'* (Rom 8:28 NIV). Wouldn't it be transforming if you truly believed and lived according to the knowledge that, *'Now to him who is able to do immeasurably more than all we ask or imagine, according to his power that is at work within in us'* (Ephesians 3:20 NIV).

Goals for Living a 'Big Life'

Having started reprogramming your self-limiting beliefs and having focused in on your God Empowering beliefs it's time to turn these into Goals for your life. It's time to choose four goals based on these beliefs. Choose four goals that will have the most dramatic transformation in your life.

For me when I first began this journey I was 30 kg over my healthy weight. I had developed some self-limiting beliefs around my appearance and influence on others, and my own self esteem. So for me I was able to turn these self-limiting beliefs into a goal, 'Lose weight - exercise 1/2 hour every day and eat healthy'.

Obviously it wasn't as simple as setting the goal; it was spending time organising my life to make it possible. I committed to meeting this goal each day and kept a journal of how I met my goal each day (even when I didn't). But at its heart was a driving belief that, 'I COULD LOSE WEIGHT', the daily focus on the goal of losing weight became greater than the short-term pleasure of eating.

It was also important to acknowledge that I couldn't use food as an emotional crutch when I was having a stressful day. It has nothing to do with willpower and everything to do with setting a goal that, long-term, would liberate me from self-limiting beliefs and disempowering behaviours.

I can tell you that I have lost 15 of those 30 kg and believe that another 10 are on shaky ground. Why? Because I began to believe I could do it and chose a long term goal over short term pleasure and comfort.

Now it has to be said that I had a few times where I lost sight of my goal and fell into old beliefs but I had developed such a desire to be someone different, to feel differently about myself that it never took more than a day or two to find my way back to my long term goal. Having my journal to do each day and re-reading my goals each day was an essential part of my reprogramming especially when life got stressful or I was sick. Are you ready?

I've designed this book so that you can record these goals for posterity and a reminder when it gets tough. However, I would like to encourage you to buy a journal and begin a daily routine (for me I read them in the morning, but completed the journaling in the evening) of what you have done each day to meet those goals.

Mine looked like this… (actual entry)

Goal 1-Lose weight and eat healthy **Why?**

My 'New truth' - I can lose weight, I want to lose weight, be healthy and feel good about myself more than I want food to make me feel okay when I'm sad, stressed or for pleasure.

God's Truth

Ephesians 4:22-24 (NRSV) *You were taught to put away your former way of life, your old self, corrupt and deluded by its lust, and to be renewed in the spirit of your minds, and to clothe yourself with the new self, created according to the likeness of God in true righteousness and holiness.*

How?

Start my day with Jesus and coffee, 1/2 hour exercise each day and eat healthy - today I walked to work and back which was 50 min (woohoo), breakfast was good - I had eggs, lunch was good - chicken and salad, dinner was good - beef and veg, probably ate too much beef and had too many coffees today, but all in all a good day, chose my long term goal about five times today over short term pleasure - pretty pumped by it.

I had three other goals which may appear later in the book.

Take the time right now to make your goals.

My four goals

Goal 1 –

Why - The 'new truth'

God's Truth –

HOW - Practical daily steps -

My four goals

Goal 2 –

Why - The 'new truth'

God's Truth -

HOW - Practical daily steps -

My four goals

Goal 3 –

Why - The 'new truth'

God's Truth -

HOW - Practical daily steps -

My four goals

Goal 4 –

Why - The 'new truth'

God's Truth –

HOW - Practical daily steps -

Chapter 10
Our true identity

Does the Devil wear Prada? Things he doesn't want you to know.

It always comes as a surprise when I recognise it both in others and myself...the great distraction.

The Devil, that fallen angel, the one we personify with evil. His greatest achievement is convincing us that this is 'all there is'. He waves in front of us the lure of happiness in the form of possessions, fame, power and pleasure. He does a great job of keeping these carrots in front of our noses so that we are so focused on them that we never look up to see something better ahead. It is the great tragedy of so many Christian lives that they never take up their God-given calling to something better.

Their lives are consumed by materialism and worldly success. Don't misunderstand me -- material possession, wealth and success can be the gift of God when they are achieved in his purpose. Unfortunately, they often become the 'purpose' at the expense of the gift of God which is in each of us. In Matthew 6:33 Jesus speaks to his disciples and reminds them that in the midst of all of life's challenges, worries and allures we are to

'Seek first his kingdom and his righteousness, and all these things will be given to you as well.' (NIV)

The devil wants you to think that wealth, success and pleasure are sinful and things that put us in conflict with our faith. This is certainly the case when we seek them at the expense of loving God and our neighbour as ourselves. However, the truth is that if we get our priorities right and focus our lives on the things that really matter then it is God's good pleasure to fill our lives with good things.

What that Devil doesn't want us to know is 'God's Blessing'. What the Devil doesn't want you to know is who you really are. The Devil wants you to stay mired in the belief that you are not good enough for your prayers to be heard. Not good enough for God to use your life or that he is even interested in blessing you. Our Identity is found in God, not in our achievements, possessions, pleasure's or even our roles.

My Identity in God

Earlier on in this book I made reference to an ancient king in the bible, 'King Solomon'. In many ways King Solomon's search for identity is one of the best documented. I'll share part of the story found in the First Book of Kings chapters 2 and 3.

'So the kingdom was established in the hand of Solomon. Solomon made a marriage alliance with Pharaoh king of Egypt.
He took Pharaoh's daughter and brought her into the city of David until he had finished building his own house and the house of the Lord and the wall around Jerusalem. The people were sacrificing at the high places, however, because no house had yet been built for the name of the Lord.
Solomon loved the Lord, walking in the statutes of David his father, only he sacrificed and made offerings at the high places. And the king went to Gibeon to sacrifice there, for that was the great high place. Solomon used to offer a thousand burnt offerings on that altar. At Gibeon the Lord appeared to Solomon in a dream by night, and God said, "Ask what I shall give you."

And Solomon said, "You have shown great and steadfast love to your servant David my father, because he walked before you in faithfulness, in righteousness, and in uprightness of heart toward you.

And you have kept for him this great and steadfast love and have given him a son to sit on his throne this day. And now, O Lord my God, you have made your servant king in place of David my father, although I am but a little child. I do not know how to go out or come in.

And your servant is in the midst of your people whom you have chosen, a great people, too many to be numbered or counted for multitude.

Give your servant therefore an understanding mind to govern your people, that I may discern between good and evil, for who is able to govern this your great people?"

It pleased the Lord that Solomon had asked this. And God said to him, "Because you have asked this, and have not asked for yourself long life or riches or the life of your enemies, but have asked for yourself understanding to discern what is right, behold, I now do according to your word.

Behold, I give you a wise and discerning mind, so that none like you has been before you and none like you shall arise after you.

I give you also what you have not asked, both riches and honour, so that no other king shall compare with you, all your days.

And if you will walk in my ways, keeping my statutes and my commandments, as your father David walked, then I will lengthen your days."

And Solomon awoke, and behold, it was a dream. Then he came to Jerusalem and stood before the ark of the covenant of the Lord, and offered up burnt offerings and peace offerings, and made a feast for all his servants.'
(ESV)

Solomon was only a young man when he became king, and his sense of identity was unformed. What he did know was the legacy his father had left and the teaching his father David had followed.

Solomon had watched his Father lead his people with integrity and humility before God. So in a dream God asks Solomon to ask for anything and it would be given to him.

Solomon aspires to be a good King and asks for the wisdom to rule his people justly. For a young man searching for identity this is an extraordinary request.

God honours and celebrates his request by also blessing him with all the things we humans crave. God blessed him with wealth, power, fame and long life. This is what Jesus was talking about in Matthew 6:33 - we are to seek what God values first and he will bless us with the other things we need to get on in life. What does God value? What does it mean to seek God's righteousness? What does it mean to seek his kingdom first? In Solomon's case he sought God's Kingdom by wanting to rule justly and teaching the people to know God's righteousness.

What does seeking God's kingdom and righteousness look like in your life? I would argue that it's all about our sense of identity, our sense of self.

I was asked recently to describe my perfect life. What would I be doing and why? What would my goals be? Where would I live? Who would it be with and why? What would my typical day look like in my perfect life.

This is not as easy as it seems. Oh sure you could compare it to your favourite holiday but that would not be real. You still have to earn a living, pay the bills, deal with all life's challenges.

The exercise was really about comparing what you wish you could do with what you were actually doing. Obviously for most of us including me there were some big discrepancies. What was interesting for me was I was able to draw on an abiding sense of Identity in God.

For me much of my perfect life centre's around living out my sense of calling and living according to the perfect plan set out for my life by Jesus. Even more surprising to me was just how much of my current life reflects my perfect life (more holidays was missing - just saying).

I probably shouldn't have been surprised but I realised that money, possessions, comfort, holidays, pleasure were not at the front of my thinking about my perfect life. Yet I have most of these things in a healthy measure. I didn't strive for them yet I have them. It seems that in seeking my identity in God and living out my calling I was still being blessed with a house, car, holidays, money. I was living Matthew 6:33 through the Grace of God.

So many of the imbalances in our life are centred around our failure to 'seek first God's kingdom and righteousness'.

Let's get something straight
We need to understand that God desires to walk with us in friendship. He desires to reconcile us to himself through Jesus. God desires to bless us as we honour Jesus in our lives. If we seek the things that really matter to God and put them first in our lives it is his good pleasure to meet our daily needs in abundance.

God is not opposed to wealth, success, ambition, fame, power, sex, joy, alcohol, or **almost** all the things we associate with pleasure or enjoyment in life. What God is opposed to is defining your life's ambition by them.

Remember it was God who invented sex and gave us the desire to succeed. God is ambitious for us so why wouldn't we be ambitious in life. However, these things are secondary to seeking the things that God values most highly. What does God call us to seek first then? What are the things God values most highly? What is his kingdom and righteousness?

What does God ask of me? When I hear this question asked it's often with a sense of frustration. Many of us think that what God asks of us is either too hard or in competition with the rest of our lives. To be really honest for some of us this is true at least on the surface. 'Jackson', a friend of mine, felt early in life that God was calling him to be a missionary.

Most of us hear the word 'missionary' and we think 'darkest Africa living in huts and poverty'. Admittedly this is true for some but this is the exception not the rule. Jackson certainly associated the call to mission work along these lines and became quite troubled by it. He made the decision that in order to become a missionary he would have to make his fortune first, then he could afford to take up this sacrificial ministry. For the next 20 years I watched Jackson move from one get-rich quick scheme to the next. Inevitably all failed with the occasionally small win. It wasn't till much later in life that Jackson discovered he had it backwards.

It's true that the call to mission is sometimes in a faraway country but more often it's right where God first called us.

Jackson was a scientist by training and had a love for all things mysterious and cosmic in our universe. While he was trying to get rich he discovered he could make money teaching teenagers and sharing all things mysterious in the universe. Finally, the 'penny dropped'. He could use his love of science to make God known through the wonders of the universe. The intricate, the amazing, the unexplainable, the order in chaos.

As Jackson began to see himself on a mission to make God known to a generation starving for an authentic knowledge of God he found great purpose and Joy. His greatest surprise was that his calling didn't require money because he got paid to teach and his greatest regret was that he hadn't first sought God's kingdom all those years ago. Jackson has become a missionary right back where he began.

So the question remains...what does God ask of me? It's simple, 'Seek first God's kingdom and his righteousness'. How do we do this? Another clue we find is in Mark 12:30-31,'you shall love the Lord your God with all your heart, and with all your soul, and with all your mind, and with all your strength. The second is this, 'You shall love your neighbour as yourself.'.

My shape and overcoming others' expectations

Most of us suffer from an overpowering sense that we are not good enough. By this I mean there is always someone in our life we wish we were more like. Perhaps we wish we could sing like that or dance like that.

They seem to make friends so easily - I wish I could write like that...Now I would like to say this can change, but truthfully we will always suffer a little from these kinds of regrets. No matter how talented or beautiful we are there will always be someone better, it's the nature of life.

Even world record holders know that eventually someone will surpass them. Given that this is the reality we all have to live with, is there a way to be 'okay' or healthy in the midst of this? Yes, there is.

Step 1 Abandon the injustice

It's very natural to feel hard done by when others around you shine with gifts they were born with. It's natural even to envy the success stories around you. However, envy can be a poison to the soul and a misplaced sense of injustice can disempower you from becoming all that God intended.
So here it is...'**yes, it's unfair**' you do deserve to sing like that, you do deserve to look that good, you do deserve to be rich and fabulous. But here's the real question - does your envy and sense of injustice serve you in any good way? Does your grief and sense of being wronged by life's deal enrich your life?
We all know the answer is No!!! Yes, it might feel good to whine about it or even wallow a little in our own self-pity but ultimately we know it just drags us down.
So let's agree to gaze longingly only occasionally and wallow in self-pity only briefly, let's agree to get on with being 'the best version of me' and let those other awful, beautiful, talented people get on with their being them. Not convinced?
Truthfully it's not injustice anyway.
What I have found to be true with my own humble gifts is that they bring both blessing and curse. A beautiful woman is adored for her beauty but struggles to be valued for her mind or her personality. A wealthy man is surrounded by people desperate to be part of his life but is never sure whether any would be with him if he were poor.

A successful woman is often hated for standing above the pack more than loved for her leadership. A man with courage who stands up for moral truth will find he is judged as a 'hater' by those with a different morality.

There is an old saying, 'The grass is always greener on the other side of the fence'. It is human nature to hunger for what we don't have but it is also a source of great unhappiness. Again I am not arguing that we can let go of all such jealousy or regret but I am suggesting that we can abandon our sense that it is 'unjust'.

Truthfully someone else's gifts, talents, looks, capacities come at a price for them personally in the same way that yours do. The healthy perspective is to say, 'I'm just me and I need to nurture what I've been given not lament what I haven't'. Living with a heightened sense of injustice, envy, jealousy, regret, self-hate because of what others have been given and what we wish we had only destroys us and gives our enemy a powerful weapon against us. Still not convinced?

I love the words of the Psalmist, *'For it was you who formed my inward parts; you knit me together in my mother's womb. I praise you, for I am ... wonderfully made. Wonderful are your works; that I know very well.* Psalm 139:13-14 (NRSV).

The psalmist never mentions his talents or his looks or his capacity; he simply acknowledges that he is a creation of wonderful intention and the God who made him did so with unfathomable thought and wonder. When we compare ourselves to others or lament what we did not receive we actually deny the powerful truth that you were uniquely created.

There is no one on this planet who looks like you, thinks like you, has your particular mix of gifts and abilities. You are wonderfully made by a wonderful God. Our journey through life is to embrace our wonderful design and become all that only 'you' can be. For us to do this we must abandon regret, injustice and lament for what we are not. You are 'amazing', 'unique', 'God's gift' if you can allow yourself to believe it.

Step 2 Reject the shape others impose on you

For certain, some of us are saying, 'I know my shape. I'm tall, I'm short, I'm round, I'm wiry'. However, I'm referring to your life's purpose rather than what you look like. The quality of our lives will be determined by how much or how little we embrace our God-given shape. As I've mentioned before I'm a pastor of a church and have spent years helping others find their God-given shape; however, I continue to explore my own.

For me, discovering my shape has been painful and difficult. I wish someone had written this book and given it to me 20 years ago. I like to think I could have avoided some of the hardships I've had with more wisdom.

Like most pastors I chose this calling or it chose me (not sure which is right), because I wanted others to know the transforming love of God. I wanted the lost, the lonely, the sick and the helpless to discover the Grace and love of Jesus and I believed I could be part of growing God's kingdom. Like most young men I believed I could do it better than the pastors I had known (Oh how ignorant and arrogant I was).

What I discovered was that God's people also wanted me to be perfect, with a perfect family, constantly inspiring sermons, boundless energy and devotion to the sick and the dying while being a humble enough servant to sweep the floor after every event and take pay cuts whenever the church was skint.

I found my every failing was up for discussion at women's guild meetings. The standard hilarious joke was that I only worked one day a week (while feeling exhausted by long hours) and having to laugh so as not to seem defensive. I was constantly compared to the pastors before me who had all miraculously become living saints having always visited them at home.

I think you get the idea. I was constantly living with failed expectations. As you could imagine as a young pastor this was a huge blow to my self-esteem and I began to think I was both a failure and the worst pastor that God had ever called to serve the church. This despite running a very successful growing church. On more than one occasion I came close to walking away from my calling and the church.

A sense of pointlessness and performance anxiety stalked me for years and the enemy constantly reminded me of the other pastors around me who were doing a better job than me. Yet I was so stubborn that for years I persisted in being what people wanted me to be rather than who God had shaped me to be.

Thankfully I've been on a journey of healing for some years now and am living and serving God more in the way I was shaped rather than who people expected me to be. I would like to say I am free from the doubts and temptation to live up to people's unrealistic expectations, but I'm not. Thankfully I'm more aware when it's happening and I work at rejecting it early rather than later.

I now collect people around me who have the gifts that I lack and they enjoy doing the ministry that used to break me. I will always have to endure the arrogance and ignorance of some who feel they are entitled to criticise me because they put money in the plate; however, I have come to understand that it's not their expectations that I have to live up to, it is instead the ones I set for myself that matter.

Step 3 Discover your shape
Recently I spent some time with a mother who lost an adult child a few years earlier. She said that her Joy died when her child died. Only a parent who's lost a child can identify with such powerful grief, however this statement is fundamentally untrue unless we make it true. Our identity and purpose in life is truly found in understanding the eternal nature of our existence.

We are made in the image of God and created to express both Joy and grief as well as to know life and death. When we put our faith in Jesus we understand that those who die in Christ will be raised to eternal life. Essentially our grief and loss are real but they are also temporal and will one day be replaced with Joy and laughter. For those who trust in Jesus our joy can be temporarily overwhelmed by grief and loss but it can never be permanently lost or destroyed.I love King David's Psalm 30 written after recovery from serious illness which was first read at the Dedication of the new Temple.

David captures the unquenchable nature of God's Joy at work in human hearts.

I will exalt you, Lord,
for you lifted me out of the depths
and did not let my enemies gloat over me.

Lord my God, I called to you for help,
and you healed me.
You, Lord, brought me up from the realm of the dead;
you spared me from going down to the pit.
Sing the praises of the Lord, you his faithful people;
praise his holy name.
For his anger lasts only a moment,
but his favour lasts a lifetime;
weeping may stay for the night,
but rejoicing comes in the morning.
When I felt secure, I said,
"I will never be shaken."
Lord, when you favoured me,
you made my royal mountain[c] stand firm;
but when you hid your face,
I was dismayed.
To you, Lord, I called;
to the Lord I cried for mercy:
"What is gained if I am silenced,
if I go down to the pit?
Will the dust praise you?
Will it proclaim your faithfulness?
Hear, Lord, and be merciful to me;
Lord, be my help."
You turned my wailing into dancing;
you removed my sackcloth and clothed me with joy,
that my heart may sing your praises and not be silent.
Lord my God, I will praise you forever.
(NIV)

Our God given shape is not defined solely by our experiences or our Genes. Our shape is defined by our unique 'one of a kind' connection to the living God.

There is no one like you, there is no one connected to God the way you can be. God has given you gifts and talents, passions, ambitions in a combination unique to you. This is why we must never seek to define our shape by what others are doing or have done. When we seek to copy or be like others we diminish the gift of God within us.

This is not to say that we cannot be inspired by others or even follow in others' callings and ministries.

It is to say that when we follow others it is to add to what they are doing, not copy it. As God's kingdom we are the ultimate 'fantasy team'.

When Christians join forces adding our unique gifts, talents, capacities to one another, we become the very expression of God's will on earth. We become the 'Church' - the visible outworking of God's Spirit at work in humankind.

Too often people say to me, 'I don't have any gifts or talents'. This is also an untrue statement. It may be true to say you haven't figured out what your gifts and talents are. Interestingly those around you (who genuinely love you) could probably tell you what they are. What is true is that this is part of the journey of discovery all Christians must take - discovering their gifts and talents and then using them to fulfil God's calling on their life.

Chapter 11
Choose life, choose love

Expand My World

Why is it that some of us seem to achieve so much? Why do we admire people who climb mountains, write novels, become rich or famous? We read autobiographies of amazing people like Nelson Mandela and Desmond Tutu, we cheer our sporting heroes as they reach into that special place that makes winners. We observe them from afar and wonder if we could ever do something amazing like them; or perhaps we lament not having the kind of skills or talent to chase our dream like they have.

Often these people we admire or aspire to be have 'a large World'. Their vision of their life is enlarged, their capacity to reach beyond their borders is great. Here is the really unsurprising truth about these people's lives; they started small.

They, like the rest of us, were mostly of humble origins with a small vision of the world and very little influence over others. You might suggest that they were no different to you and me, except for one thing.

They believed in their ability to expand their world, they believed that they had something to offer the world in which they lived. Some of the greatest people of history expanded their world even in the face of a world that rejected them or pushed back at them.

At this point you're probably expecting me to say something like, 'They believed in themselves' or 'They chased their dream', but these are unhelpful clichés for average Joes like you and me because quite often they were extraordinary people.

No matter how hard I might train to be an elite football player I'm not going to play for Manchester United; I've never had the genetics for it. So my point is not, 'If you set your mind to it you can achieve anything' because it's not true. My point is this; life is less about what we achieve or how great we become but simply how well we can 'Expand our World'. Let me explain...

Malcolm was a good golfer from a young age and was a celebrated club champion. He decided from a young age to pursue a PGA card and successfully enrolled in the PGA training program.

He achieved well and played in many regional PGA events but was never able to reach the heights he had dreamed of and worked so hard for. He loved golf and realised if he wanted to continue to pursue a career in golf he would have to find another way to enlarge his world.

He wasn't going to 'cut it' as a golf pro on the tour so what could he do? In exploring his options, he realised his other love for golf was in sharing his knowledge of the game. He expanded his world again by training as a golf pro/coach.

He now coaches the next generation of hopefuls and continues to believe that his world can be expanded as he pours himself into the next champion.

In that moment of 'I'm not going to make it on the tour' Malcolm had a choice to shrink his world or grow it. He could have become resentful about chances he wasn't given or embittered by his own failure. Instead he chose to keep expanding his world and find the place where meaning and purpose lined up with his passion. He still wishes he had made it on the tour but he is happy doing something that he loves.

Recently I've been journeying in life with Zach, a member of my church. Zach was a successful CEO of a large corporate firm and sat on the top of his world. Others looked on and admired him and sought to copy his success. Zach seemed to have a large world and his influence seemed large. At 55 Zach, still at the top of his game, had a heart attack which although he survived left him greatly weakened. In fact, it seemed to lead to a series of health issues which forced him to leave his position in the company and spend the next year in rehabilitation.

In this year his world shrank to doctors' appointments, rehab. clinic, physios, and social workers.

Zach received many well wishes in small doses by phone but became reclusive, and rejected what he felt was the pity of former colleagues and friends. Twelve months after the heart attack he was barely leaving the house.

Zach became depressed and began to drive his wife to despair as well. Thankfully he agreed to see a psychiatrist who Zach felt was unhelpful but a good idea all the same. Zach kept saying things like, 'When I'm better I'll get back into riding', 'when I'm better I'll go back to work'.

Zach's world had shrunk to the point where even though his health had recovered significantly, 12 months later he lived as if he was waiting for things to return all by themselves.

Now for a man who had achieved so much and seemed to have such a 'large world', why did his future sound so bleak? We began to talk about his shrunken world and how he might slowly grow it again. We began with small things, things that brought him Joy. Spending more time with his grandkids, playing golf again, walking, going out for dinner.

These might seem insignificant but expanding our world often happens through small choices. I remain hopeful for Zach's world to keep growing. Both Zach and Malcolm discovered that our world is as small or as large as we are willing to make it.

Our attitude and willingness to expand our territory is more important than whether we become successful or famous for what we do. The Joy of living comes from embracing the season we are in, and expanding our world within that season.

Waiting for others to do it, or for our health to improve, or our luck to change, or whatever other excuse we might use will only shrink our world. The question to ask each day is, 'In what small way can I enlarge my world today'?

I can't write a novel because who would read it? Write it anyway - you'll be proud of yourself and expand your world.

I could never learn a language. It's too hard. Enrol in a class - you might surprise yourself and expand your world. I can't go to Europe, what if the plane crashes? When I was young a friend of mine died when the hammock he was in pulled a wall down on him. We can't live in fear of what might happen; this only shrinks our world. Adventure awaits us when we face our fear of death and failure. Embrace the opportunities your season offers you even if they are small and insignificant. Success isn't our objective, embracing our life is.

Choose Life, Choose Love
Living the pastor's life with hundreds of people critiquing your preaching, teaching and choices can be pretty intimidating and trying to live up to expectations of perfection is impossible.

However, there is a really important flip side to the story of a pastor's life. The flip side is the people who love you, support you, encourage you, those who celebrate your preaching and teaching, those who walk with you in serving God and his kingdom, those who will correct you and speak honestly in your life from a place of love, not judgement. Learning to choose which voices will be more powerful in your life is critically important.

The average pastor only lasts five years in ministry for many of the reasons I've stated. However, I bet there were people in their lives that were encouraging and supporting them. So my question is…which voices triumphed? I have been on this roller coaster my whole ordained life. Sometimes the detractors drove me away; sometimes my supporters nurtured me to stay. The most important day on the roller coaster was the day I decided to do it all for love. The day I chose love was the day I chose life.

What do you mean?

It's simple really: we will all have people in our lives who speak negativity into us through words and actions. Sadly, they are sometimes people who are meant to love and encourage us. In some cases, there is little we can do about this other than limit their opportunities to speak or act negatively in our lives.

Sometimes people are unaware they are doing it and confronting them about the problem can bring about change but equally sometimes it is necessary to end relationships. Perhaps it is your boss or a shareholder - these people sometimes speak negatively into our lives and there is nothing we can do about it. There is however a surprising power we have, even in the face of unequal power-sharing relationships.

My journey with love began at the age of 18 when Jesus revealed himself to me. When he entered my life I had no idea how broken I really was. Growing up, I was subject to emotional and sexual abuse and I grew up with a distorted view of love. In fact, what I thought was love wasn't love at all. It's a painful story to tell and probably doesn't serve any other purpose here than to say I had some negative and destructive voices speaking into my life.

As a brand new Christian I was still filled with hate and rage toward those who had hurt me over many years. God began a healing journey with me; however, I was a Christian for two years before I truly began a journey of healing for my past.

I remember, after attending church one night, feeling like I was trapped in a deep pit with no light. I felt so lost in my hate and my non-existent self-esteem. Then in a waking dream a light shone into the darkness of my pit. In the light was Jesus wearing sunglasses.

He took off the glasses and handed them to me and said, 'Put them on. From now on view yourself through my eyes; these are your Jesus-coloured sunglasses'. This powerful metaphor has been a guiding light in my life. Whenever I struggle with self-worth I remember how Jesus sees me.

Yet to all who did receive him, to those who believed in his name, he gave the right to become children of God. (John 1:12 NIV)
I no longer call you servants, because a servant does not know his master's business. Instead, I have called you friends, for everything that I learned from my Father I have made known to you. (John 15:15 NIV)

According to Jesus my heavenly father calls me his child an adopted son, and Jesus calls me his friend. Both of these affirmations speak of complete forgiveness and acceptance.

"My prayer is not for them alone. I pray also for those who will believe in me through their message, that all of them may be one, Father, just as you are in me and I am in you. May they also be in us so that the world may believe that you have sent me. (John 17:20-21 NIV)

Through Jesus I am one with God the Father, loved by God the Father, forgiven by God the Father and made perfect by God the Father.
This knowledge redeems my broken understanding of love. This knowledge destroys self-loathing and despair. This knowledge when it finds its way into our hearts brings healing, hope and a future.

...but whoever drinks the water I give them will never thirst. Indeed, the water I give them will become in them a spring of water welling up to eternal life."
(John 4:14 NIV)

The water Jesus gives is the water of forgiveness, healing, truth and life. Whenever others criticise me (even if their criticism is true) I turn to Jesus and drink. I am not perfect, I will fail people, I will make mistakes but none of this changes the fact that I have true worth as a child of God.
My looks have no bearing on my value to God, my successes or failures do no increase or lessen my status as friend to Jesus.

When I said 'I chose love, I chose life', I meant I choose to listen to the voice of the one who gives me eternal life. I don't pretend that I don't hear or respond to the negative voices and actions in my life but I chose not to let them be walls and barriers in my life.

To the mountains of self-doubt in my life I say,
Since, then, you have been raised with Christ, set your hearts on things above, where Christ is, seated at the right hand of God.
Set your minds on things above, not on earthly things. For you died, and your life is now hidden with Christ in God. When Christ, who is your life, appears, then you also will appear with him in glory. (Colossians 3:1-4 NIV)
Choose love, choose Jesus, choose life.

Other titles available from Lakeside Publishing: check our website www.lakesidepublishing.com.au for more publications, to provide feedback and to order.

Small Group Bible Studies
Going for Growth – Stuart Webb 2012

This is a practical and easy to follow study in the need for and ways to go about sustaining growth in both our personal lives, and in that of the church. This has been a well supported book, with many study groups using it throughout Queensland.

Living a Life in Balance – Stuart Webb 2013

This study aims at enriching each person's life by focusing on a close and faithful walk with Jesus. It tackles the often talked-about issue of living by faith. In his customary practical and easy to understand manner, Fr Stuart looks at real and powerful ways in which to "increase our faith" as the disciples said.

Come to your Senses – Janet Dyke 2013

This study encourages you to, quite literally, use all your senses to worship to become aware of God in your life. As each chapter focuses in turn on hearing, sight, smell, taste and touch you are invited to use your senses to enrich your faith individually and as a community of believers.

I Believe – Janet Dyke 2014

Creeds remind us that our faith is not locked into individuality but is something we share together. This group study book challenges new Christians and seasoned travelers to reflect on Scripture and explore their faith through the Apostles Creed as they deepen their relationship with our amazing God.

Be Transformed by the Renewing of your Mind – Stuart Webb 2014

When we become Christians, we decide to follow a new path – a path chosen by God, formed by God's design to mould us to his likeness. This study series invites us to new ways of thinking and living as we respond to the work of the Holy Spirit in our minds. It will energise anyone hungry and thirsty for more of God in their lives.

HTK 28 Day Challenge – Stuart Webb 2014

When a caterpillar begins its transformation, it commits to an irreversible metamorphosis. So also, when God calls our name and we receive Jesus as our Lord and Saviour, we commit to a life-long transformation. This 28 Day Challenge asks us to commit to daily Bible reading and prayer with journaling, and a commitment to stay closely connected with Christ's body, the Church.

Tell It Like It Is – Janet Dyke 201.Have you ever thought about sharing your faith in your friend, Jesus, who is the Lord and Saviour of the world, but you just don't know how to begin? If so, this study may be a help. It is designed for use in small groups to help Christians of all ages and stages of their faith journey to share their faith by trusting God and sharing their own story.

God Breathed – Stuart Webb 2015

This study invites us deeper into the new life that God offers us. Irrespective of our age, God wants to renew us through a Springtime for our souls. In discovering our true identity as "God Breathed´ we become inspired again to pursue our new life in Christ. We become "God seekers" as we open our hearts and minds to new possibilities. We start to live for God as God begins to live again in us, and in this way we become "God Empowered" to walk in his way.

The Love of God – Peter Hall 2015
Perhaps the best known verse in the New Testament in relation to God's love must be John 3:16 *For God so loved the world...* This series of six studies encourages small groups to reflect on the amazing Love of God in three ways – God's love for us, our love for God, and God's love mutually shared.

Making a Rainbow – Janet Dyke 2016
In our lives, it is not just light and water droplets that make rainbows, but also all the shades and variations of the lives of the people who share life's journey with us. This study series explores the diverse nature of Christ's body – the communion of saints of which all the redeemed are a part – that is God's church. What a wonderful effect the spectrum of our united colours can bring to a world of darkness and strife. We are indeed part of the rainbow of God's promise of love and hope in and to our world.

Inspirational

Act Justly, Love Mercy, Walk Humbly – Margaret Pearson 2015
The thoughtful poems, prayers and reflections in this inspirational book are accompanied by original artwork in glorious colour. Margaret has a heart for social justice and her love for the least and the lost is apparent as this book inspires, encourages and challenges its readers.

Fair as the Moon – Deanne Lister 2015
This anthology of inspirational poems and reflections is sure to speak to young and old of the great love of the Lord of Life. Deanne has related her own journey of discovery of God through some of the poems; as in life some are joyful, some intensely sad, expressing moments of intimacy and separation, tension and contentment, sorrow and happiness, and many more situations.

In the Quiet Place – Kate Johnson *Illustrated by Valmai Ham* 2015
This lovely and inspirational anthology was prepared by two talented Christian ladies from HTK. The poems and pencil drawings speak of God's creative and steadfast love through all of the circumstances and seasons of life.

If I ever saw a miracle ... – Frank Phillips 2015
This memoir reflects on the amazing work God has done in the author's life. The love of God in the detail of the day-to-day is inspiring and immensely encouraging. The reader is gently reminded to give the small things to God who will do amazing things with them. Nothing in our lives is too small for God to use.

Pastoral

Baptism of Children: A Parents' Guide – Peter Hall
2014

Rev Peter Hall is an ordained minister in the Uniting Church in Australia and has a particular interest in helping people understand our faith and what it means for daily living. In this workbook designed for use with families in baptism preparation, he explains baptism as an entry point into the Christian Faith, and explores what baptism means and the responsibilities that go with it.

Look for more resources for the local church coming soon from Lakeside Publishing:

- **First communion resources**
- **Apps for iPhone and Android**
- **Daily Bible study guides**
- **Small Group Bible studies**

LAKESIDE PUBLISHING

Bibliography

ESV The Holy Bible,
English Standard Version Copyright © 2001
Crossway Bibles, Good News Publishing
NIV Holy Bible, New International Version®,
NIV® Copyright ©1973, 1978, 1984, 2011
by Biblica Inc
NRSV New Revised Standard Version Bible,
copyright © 1989 the Division of Christian Education
of the National Council of the Churches of Christ
in the United States of America.

Stuart Webb is a Pastor, teacher, visionary leader and author. Lakeside bestselling Author of studies, God Breathed, Living Life in Balance, Going for Growth, HTK 28Day Spiritual challenge, Be Transformed. Stuart and his wife Michelle have four children Thomas, Emma, Harry and Isabella and live on the Sunshine coast in Queensland, Australia.

www.ingramcontent.com/pod-product-compliance
Lightning Source LLC
Chambersburg PA
CBHW072024040426
42447CB00009B/1715